Doll Couture

Handcrafted Fashions for 18-inch Dolls

All Made from Vintage Fabric

Marsha Greenberg

RUNNING PRESS
PHILADELPHIA · LONDON

Books published by Running Press are available at special discounts for bulk purchases in the United States by corporations, institutions, and other organizations. For more information, please contact the Special Markets Department at the Perseus Books Group, 2300 Chestnut Street, Suite 200, Philadelphia, PA 19103, or call (800) 810-4145, ext. 5000, or e-mail special.markets@perseusbooks.com.

ISBN 978-0-7624-5372-6
Library of Congress Control Number: 2014940376

E-book ISBN 978-0-7624-5538-6

9   8   7   6   5   4   3   2   1
Digit on the right indicates the number of this printing

Photographs by Bryan E. McCay
Designed by Melissa Gerber
Edited by Cindy De La Hoz
Typography: Bernhard Modern, Futura STD, SamWendy Bold, ITC Quorum, and Navinno Regular

Running Press Book Publishers
2300 Chestnut Street
Philadelphia, PA 19103-4371

Visit us on the web!
www.runningpress.com

This book is dedicated to
"My Brian," my loving husband
of 42 years. May we have
many more years together!

Contents

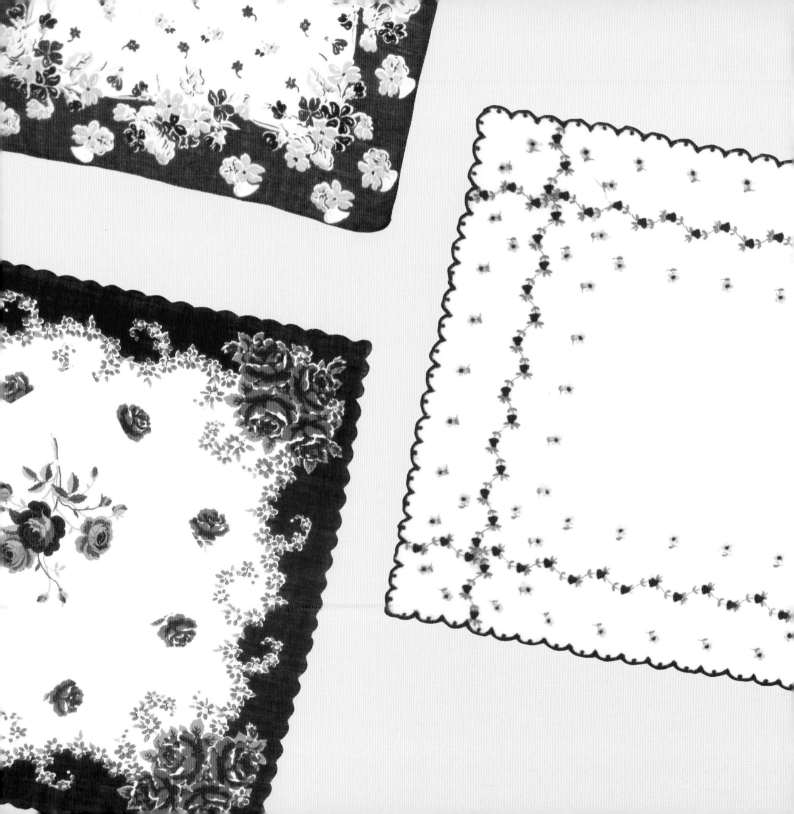

Introduction

If you have ever wondered if it is possible

to have too much fun . . . let me tell you firsthand, I think not! I enjoyed *every minute* that I spent working on the vintage couture doll dresses for this book. Designing for this 18-inch doll allowed me to utilize my lifetime collection of vintage fabrics, which in turn opened up a whole new window of creativity. I harvested everything I could find from my plethora of vintage treasures from every drawer, every closet, linen cupboard, and box!

My vintage treasure trove of goodies included: vintage tea towels, cross-stitch tablecloths, antimacassars, bedspreads, pillowcases, embroidered table runners, crochet doilies, ruffled doilies, table napkins, placemats, antique laces, curtain valances, cocktail napkins, wine glass stem coasters (see embroidered Duck dress, page 92), kitchen towels, and even an antique children's bedspread (see Circus dress with the blue elephant, page 98). And, of course, my favorite one-of-a-kind vintage hankies, crochet hankies, and embroidered hankies. I was also able to tap into my large collection of trims: satin flowers, ceramic and plastic buttons, ribbons, pearls, and jewelry to accessorize the dresses.

When I utilized only hankies to design a dress, I used a minimum of three to five hankies. One of my favorite dresses devoured *nine* embroidered hankies (the white dress with the little house on the bodice, see page 25). Many of my dresses also incorporated brand new fabrics which I twinned with their vintage "cousins."

The crochet doily dresses were an absolute delight to create from a mixed media of doilies, hankies, laces, and new fabrics. I mixed crochet doilies with *ruffled* crochet doilies to create fullness to the skirt.

I became obsessed with designing shoes to match the dresses, and what fun they were! Yes, they were a little time-consuming, but the results made me smile and they were well worth the time.

One of the reasons I love sewing so much is because I can see results quickly on something I *just* cut out and watch it take shape before my eyes! All the different pieces marry each other to form a happy union!

The sewing patterns I included in this book will work great for beginning sewers as well as advanced seamstresses. Also, the patterns can be intermingled to expand your design possibilities. I sincerely hope that this book will inspire you to create your very own vintage heirloom treasures and hope that you will have as much fun as I have had making the fashions seen in this book. There are no "rules or restrictions" here, so go ahead and leave the creativity button in the "ON" position.

Happy Sewing!

Love,

Marsha

P.S. One last thing: I had a *field day* cutting and styling the doll's hair for this book! I am sure most of us can relate to cutting your doll's hair after Mom told you not to (but we did it anyway!). It was every little girl's dream . . . "Shear" Heaven!

How to use this book

The following pages of this book are an inspirational showcase of couture for 18-inch dolls—all made from vintage fabric. Beside each doll is a small icon with a number from one through nine. Each of these numbers refer to a different pattern that has been provided in the pocket on the inside back cover of this book. To recreate any of the looks found in this book, note the number beside the doll, locate the corresponding pattern in the back of the book, and get started! Sewing instructions for these patterns begin on page 136.

Key

1 Skirt

2 Dress with Contrast Band Border

3 Circular Crochet Dress/Circular Skirt

4 Blouse

5 Romper

6 Dress with Round or Pointed Collar

7 Pin-Tuck Inset Bodice Dress

IMPORTANT NOTES:

There are many dresses throughout the book that do not have any collars. For those dresses I used embroidered hankies or the corner of a cutwork hankie to embellish the bodice front and back. You can also use lace or crochet edgings to go around the neck. Please refer to the Dress with Round or Pointed Collar dress pattern sewing instructions to create these bodices, and just omit the collar.

Similarly, some of the shoes featured in this book do not have straps, so you would simply skip the step where you add a strap when recreating those.

As hats and shoes are very obvious pieces, they have been omitted from this key, but this book includes patterns and sewing instructions for creating both of these items.

Vintage Couture Gallery

Hankie Couture girls are
cut from the cloth of
delicate persuasion.
They particularly love light
and airy hand crochet patterns,
especially in a floral design!

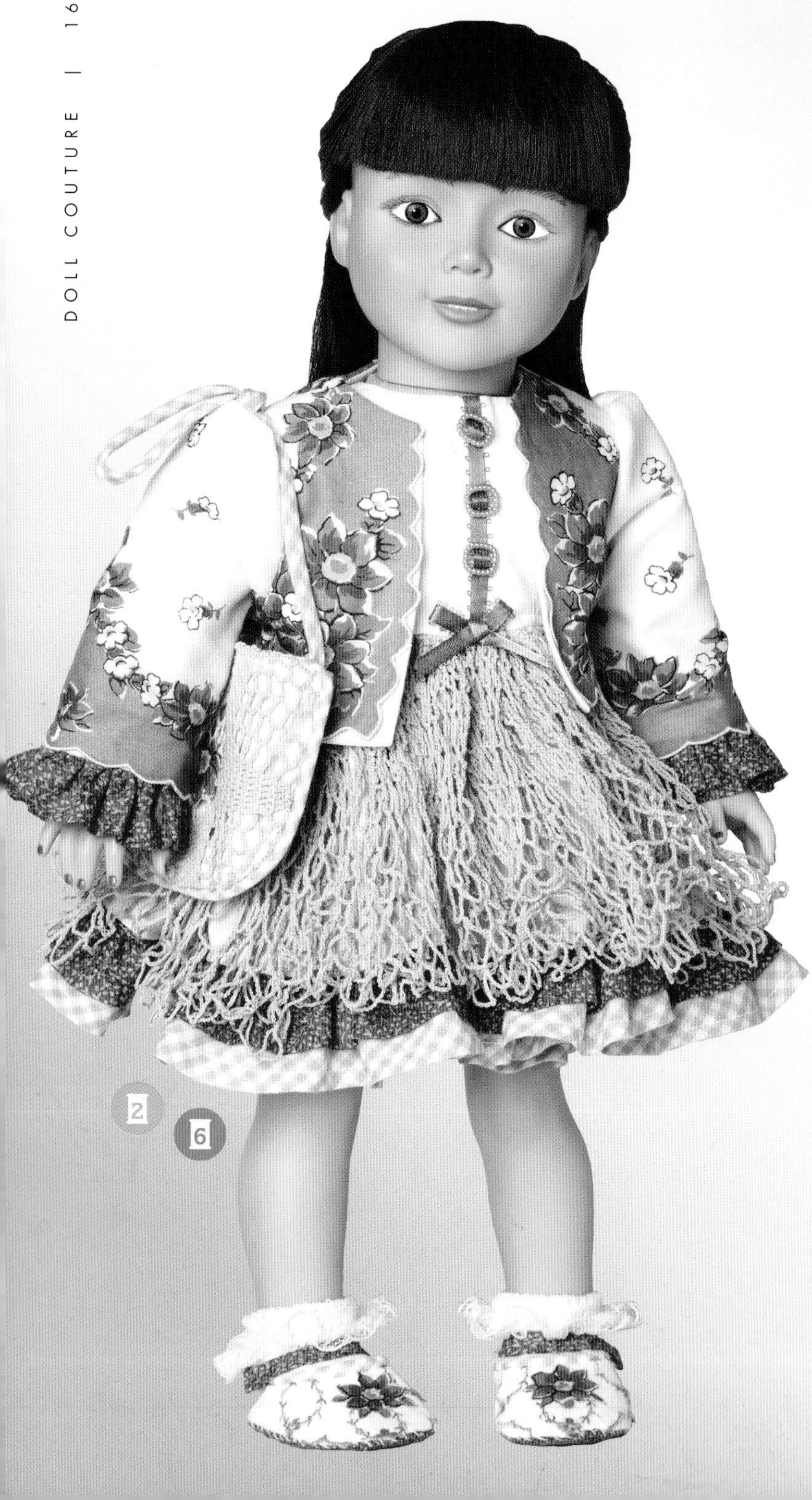

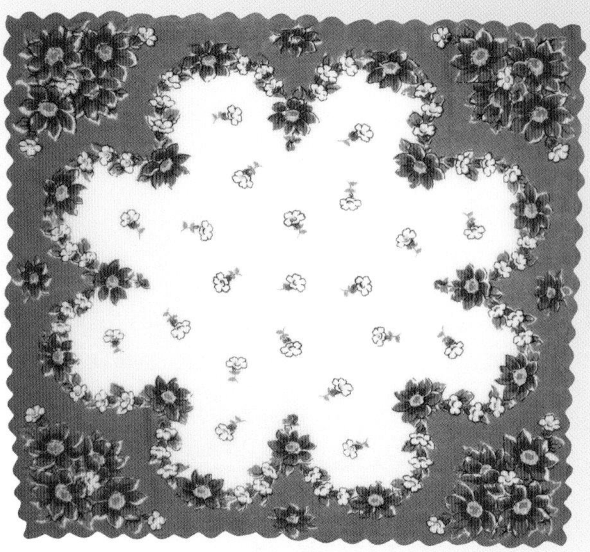

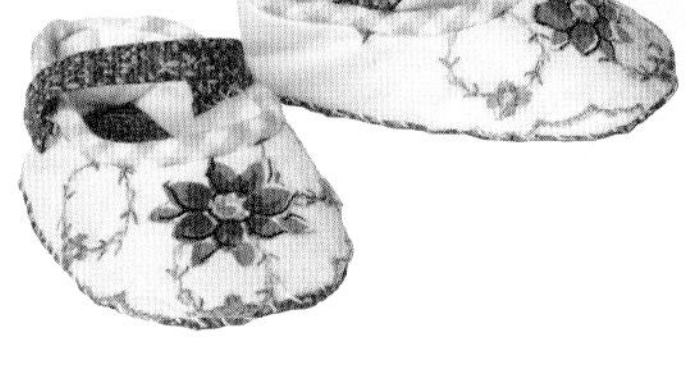

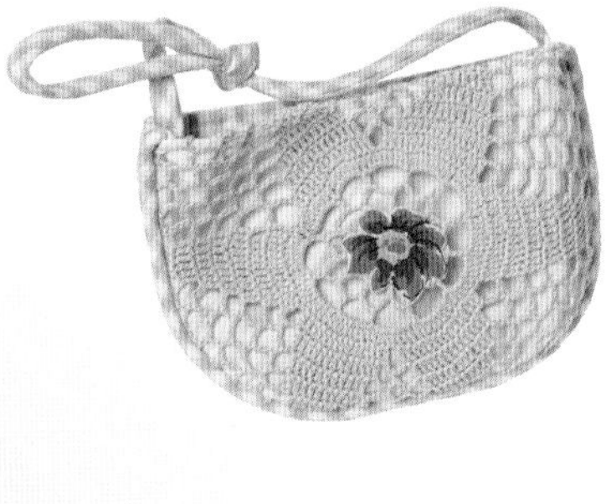

Hankie Couture girls
have a playfully expressive

lifestyle.

She begins her day with a
twinkle in her eye
and ends with the delight
of certainty!

Hankie Couture Mantra:

Keep things

fresh, simple, and chic!

The energy
of an H.C. girl delights
everyone! Her dresses are
riveting and dramatic.

3

2

Hankie Couture delights the senses.

Everything matters.

③

⑥

Others are impressed
with a Hankie Couture girl's
easy-going attitude,
which includes:
Energy that is awe-inspiring!
Enthusiasm for pretty thoughts!
Artistic flare for fun!

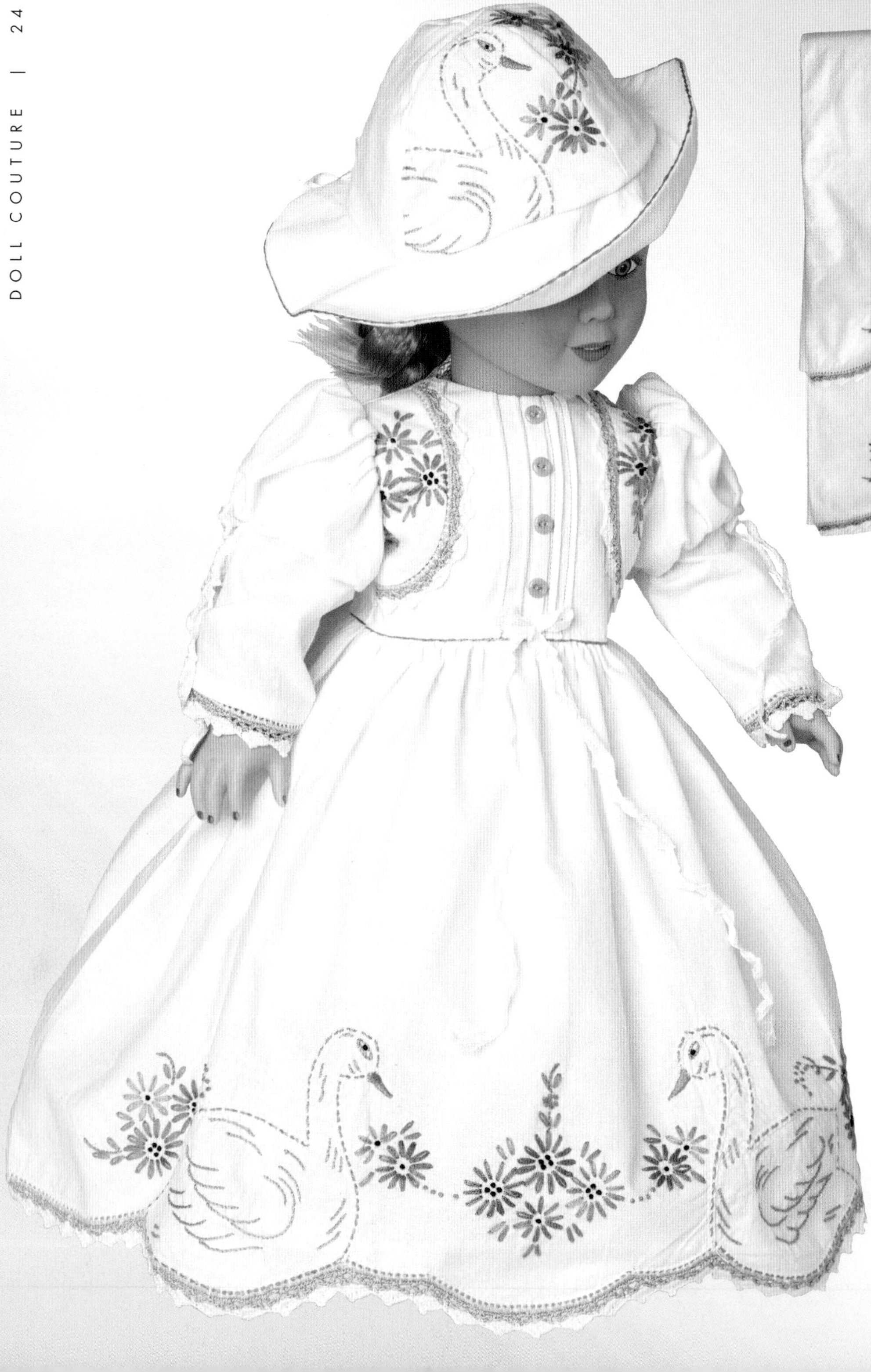

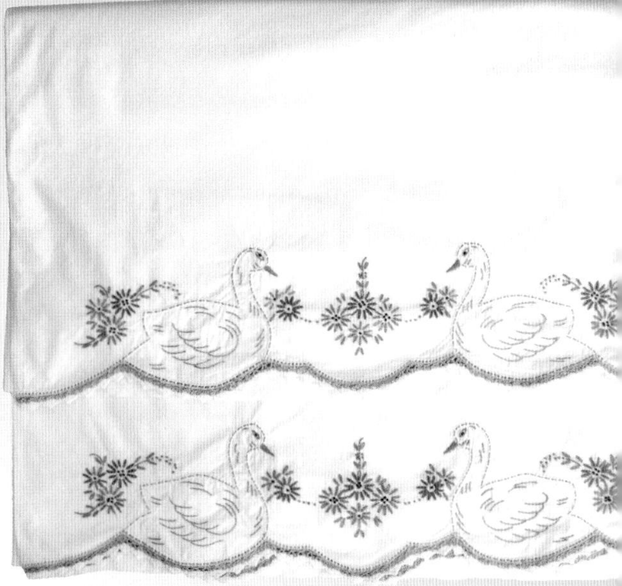

H.C. girls feel at *at home* no matter where they are.

Hankie Couture girls
know that a hankie dress
is the first ingredient for a
successful party!

Hankie Couture clothing is

beautiful,

clever, and very necessary!

H.C. girls are prone to huge

enthusiasm!

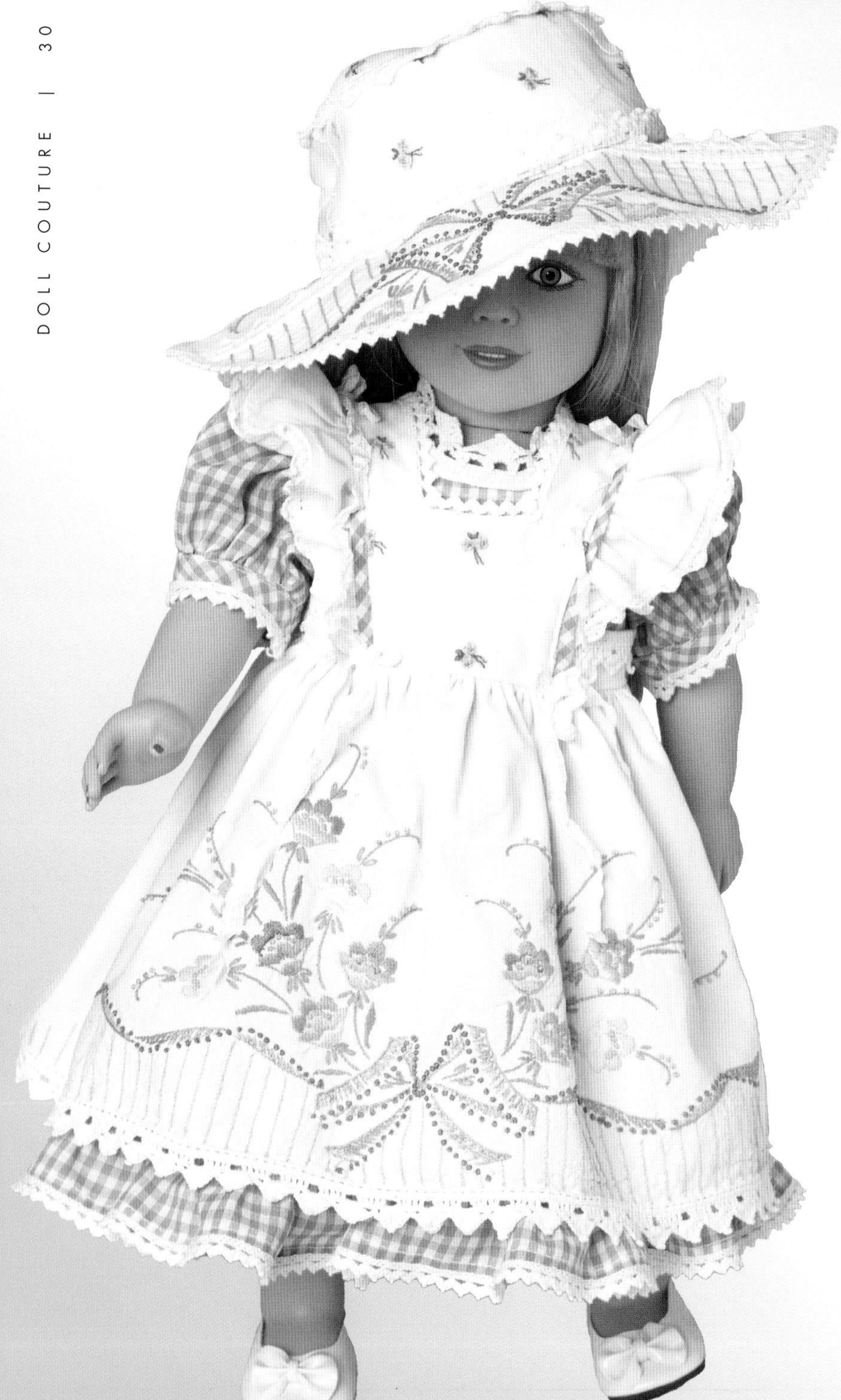

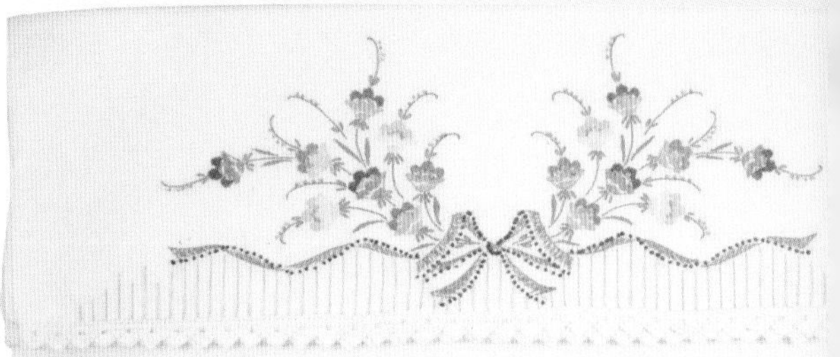

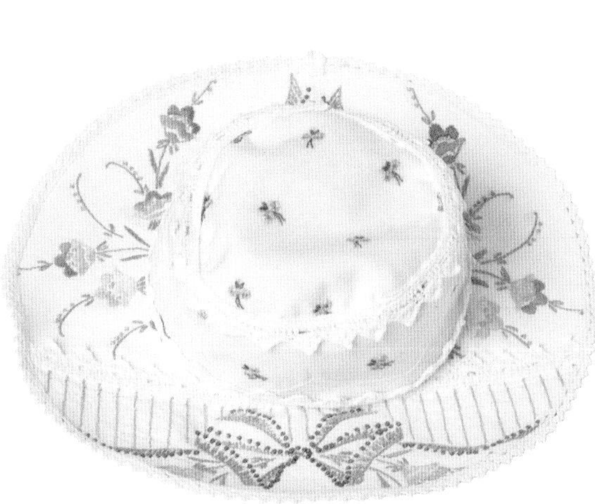

Hankie Couture: That's the
beauty of it!

New shoes? Check!

New hat? Check!

New Attitude?

Check!

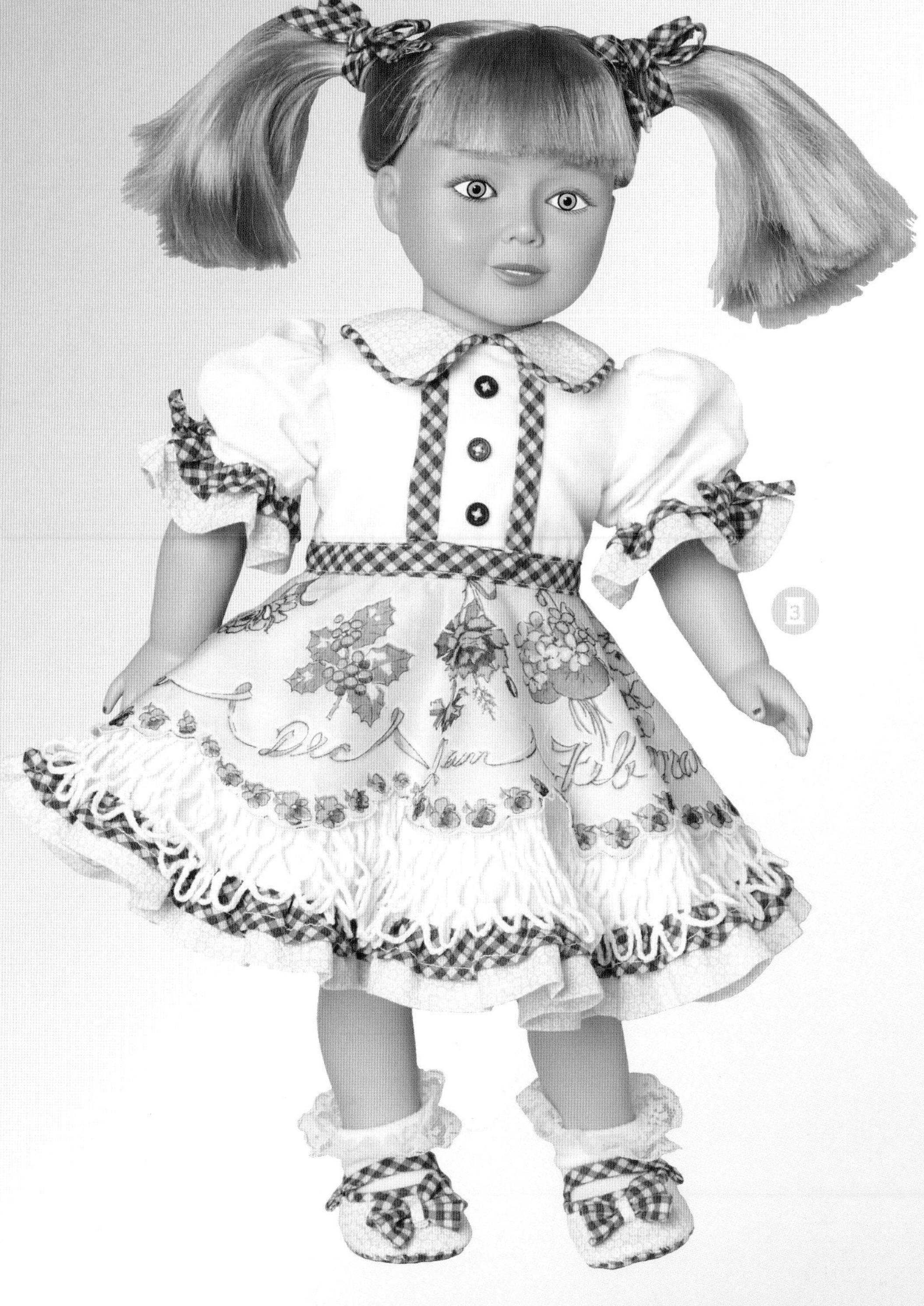

3

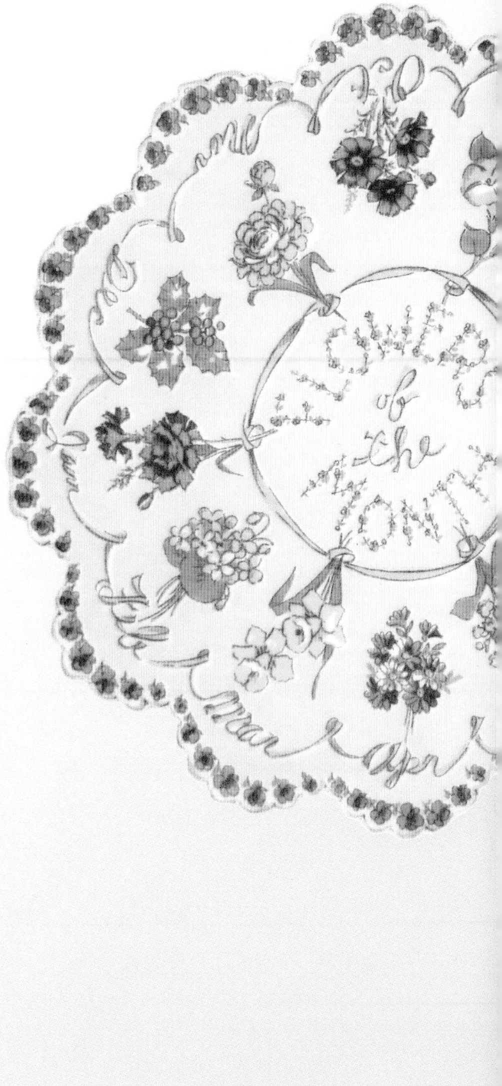

A Hankie Couture gal finds

beautiful inspiration

in whimsical patterns.

3

She has a
great respect
for all living things!

Hankie Couture Mental Chemistry
for making things work:
Alter it. Tweak it. Fix it. Fine-tune it.

Finish it!

The spice of the
imagination feeds a Hankie
Couture girl's appetite.

She loves to eat!

Hankie Couture Factoid:

A positive perspective

shines through everything she does.

H.C. girls stand out in their
own sophisticated, subtle way.
They bring their gifts of
smiles to all.

In the world of Hankie Couture,
the girls know how to make a
favorable impression:
be sincere and honest.

Hankie Couture girls like to get all
dolled up!

Hankie Couture girls
are of the opinion
that long holidays are
good for the soul!

Hankie Couture girls
are very wise! They
make an effort
to learn something
new every day.

⑥ ⑦

A few simple rules about
wearing Hankie Couture:
Be spontaneous,
think pretty thoughts,
have fun!

Hankie Couture
Rules of Etiquette:
Lend an ear.
Provide a helping hand.
Be humble.

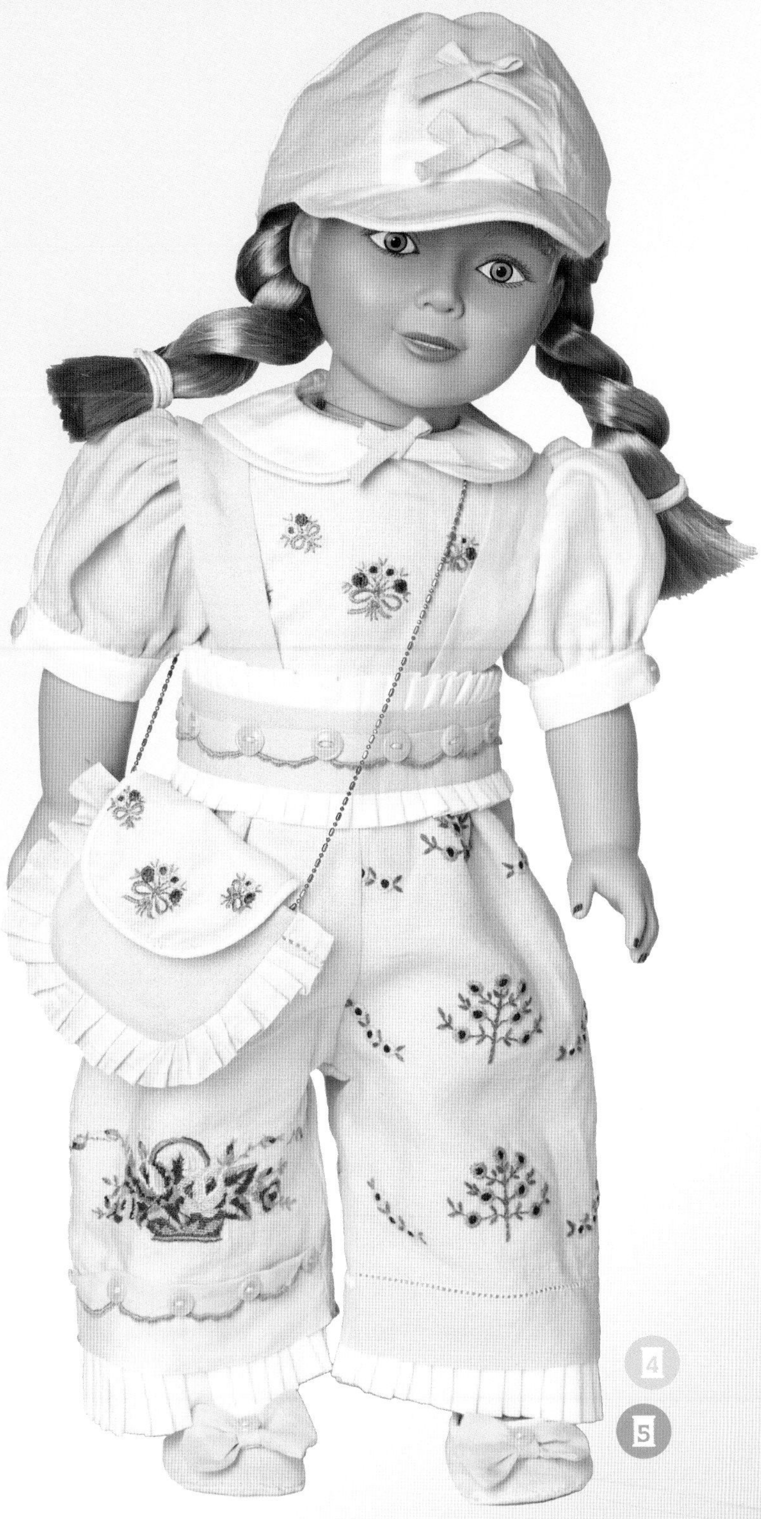

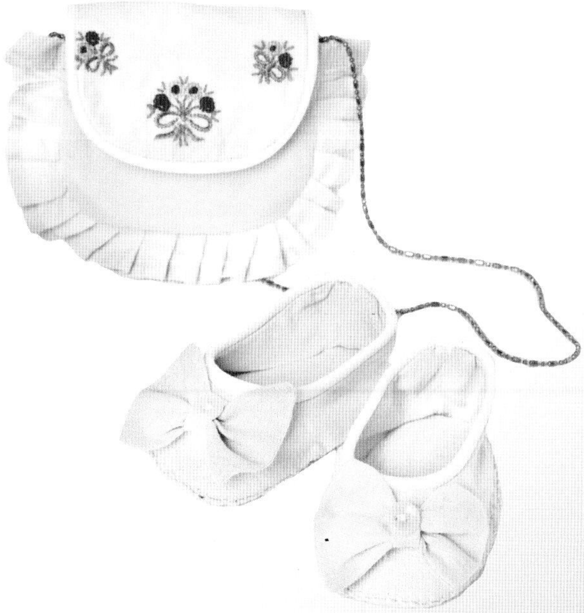

4

5

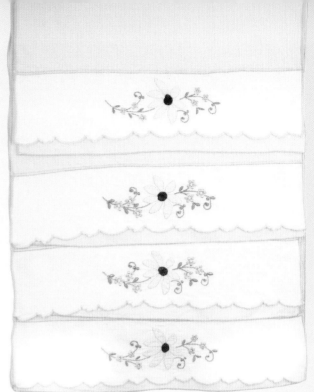

7

Hankie Couture world:
The kind you
daydream about!

The girls of Hankie
Couture like to
keep the windows of
wisdom
and kindness wide open.

3
6

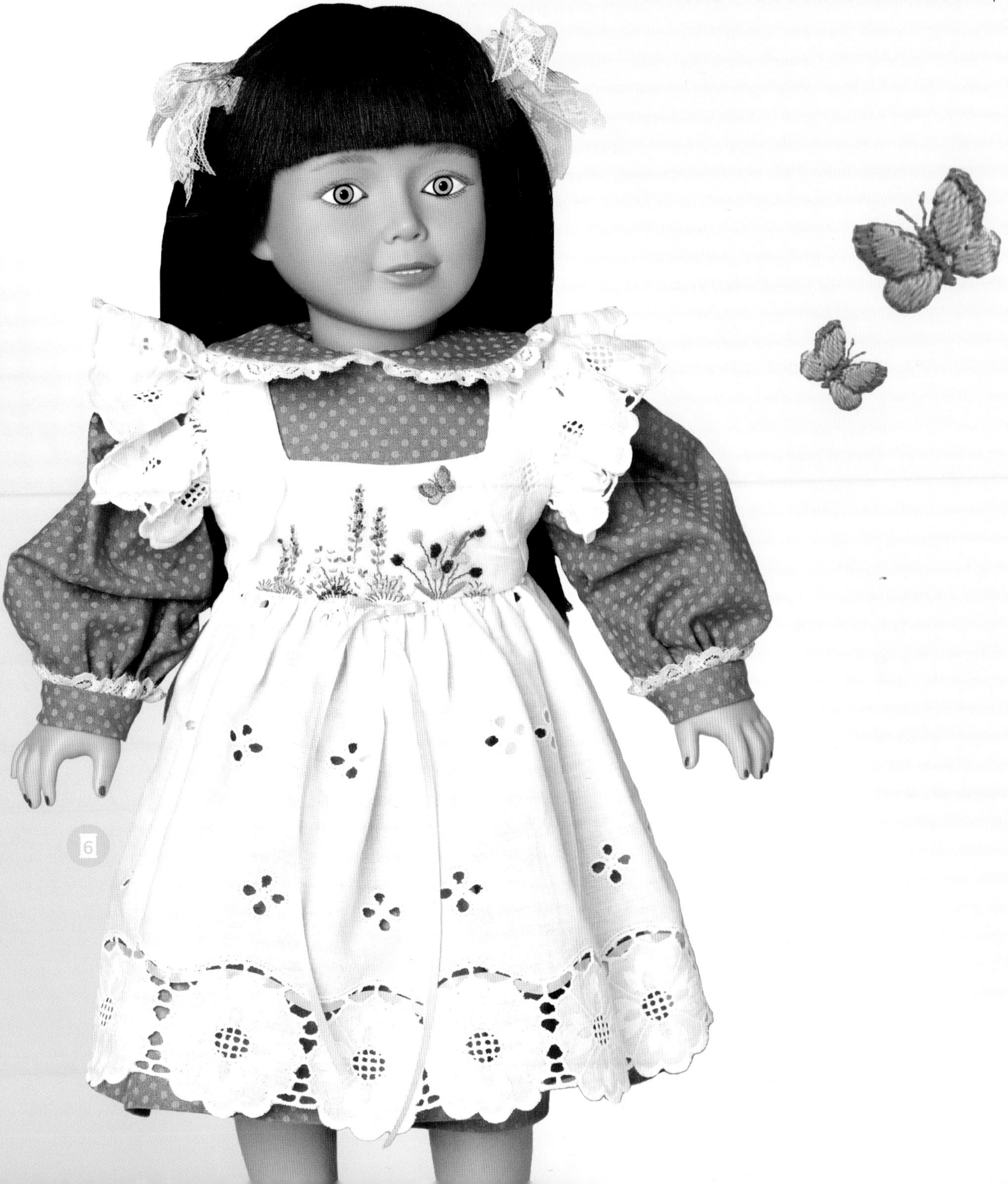
6

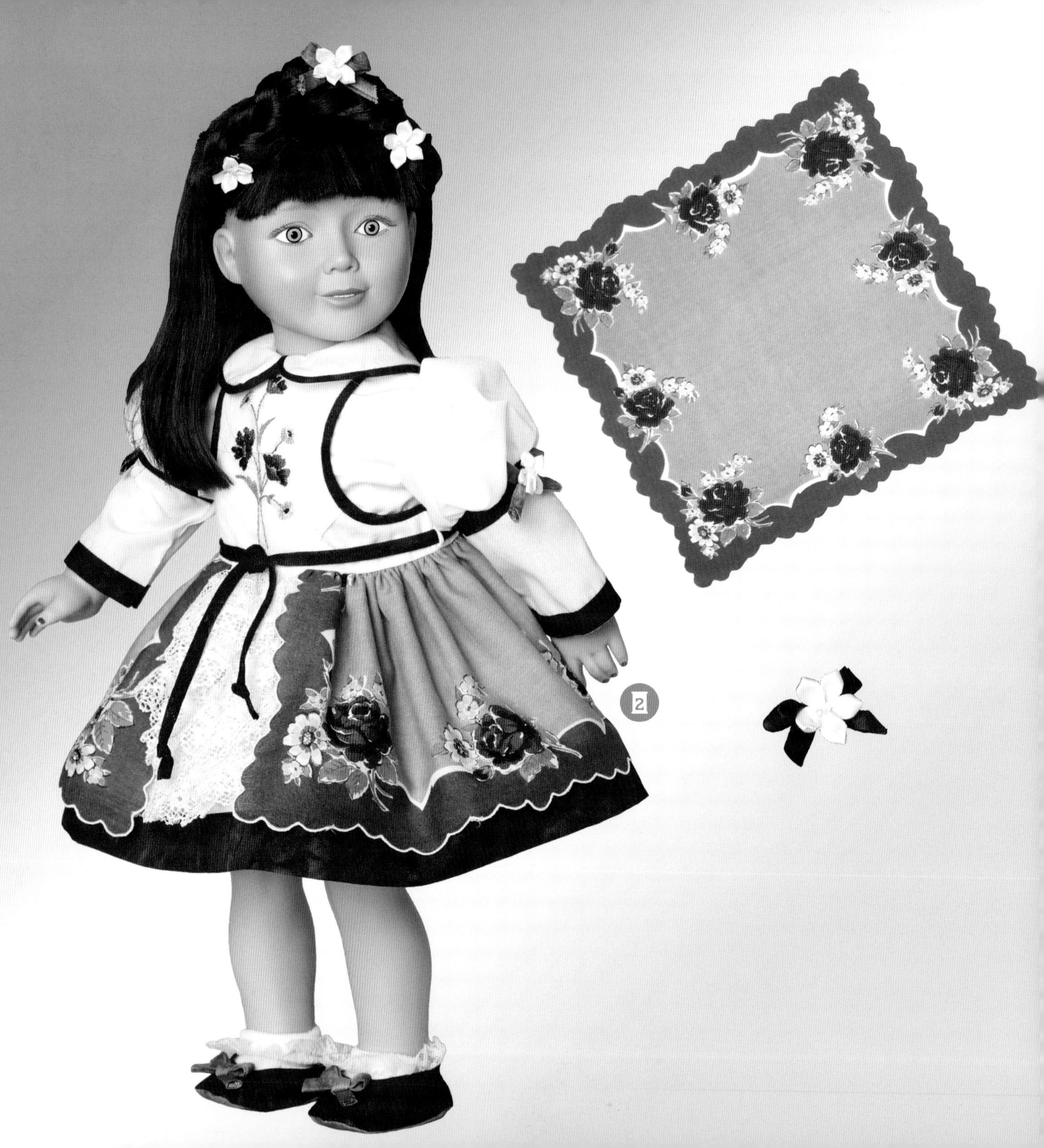

Admission into the world
of Hankie Couture depends
on two things:

Being grateful

for what one has and simple acts of

kindness.

Hankie Couture girls
are dazzled
by the ordinary!

Hankie Couture girls believe in
creating value
in their everyday lives:
They strive to make their deeds
and actions count.

Home

is where you find joy.

Hankie Couture girls
jump at any opportunity to
do a good deed.

The girls of Hankie

Couture make time for

free-spirited

fun and beloved activities!

The daughters of Hankie
Couture easily succumb to
the charms
of a profusion of color.
They draw energy from nature's
brilliant kaleidoscope.

Hankie Couture girls
are reckless with
creativity.
They are architects of fashion,
and quietly superb!

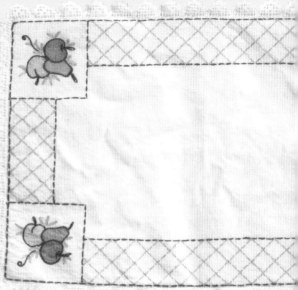

Hankie Couture young ladies
have a winning attitude:
They feel wonderfully
alive when they are being
creative.

It is definitely spring here,
in the world of Hankie Couture.
The weather is fabulous and all
of nature's creatures are off to an
exhilarating start!

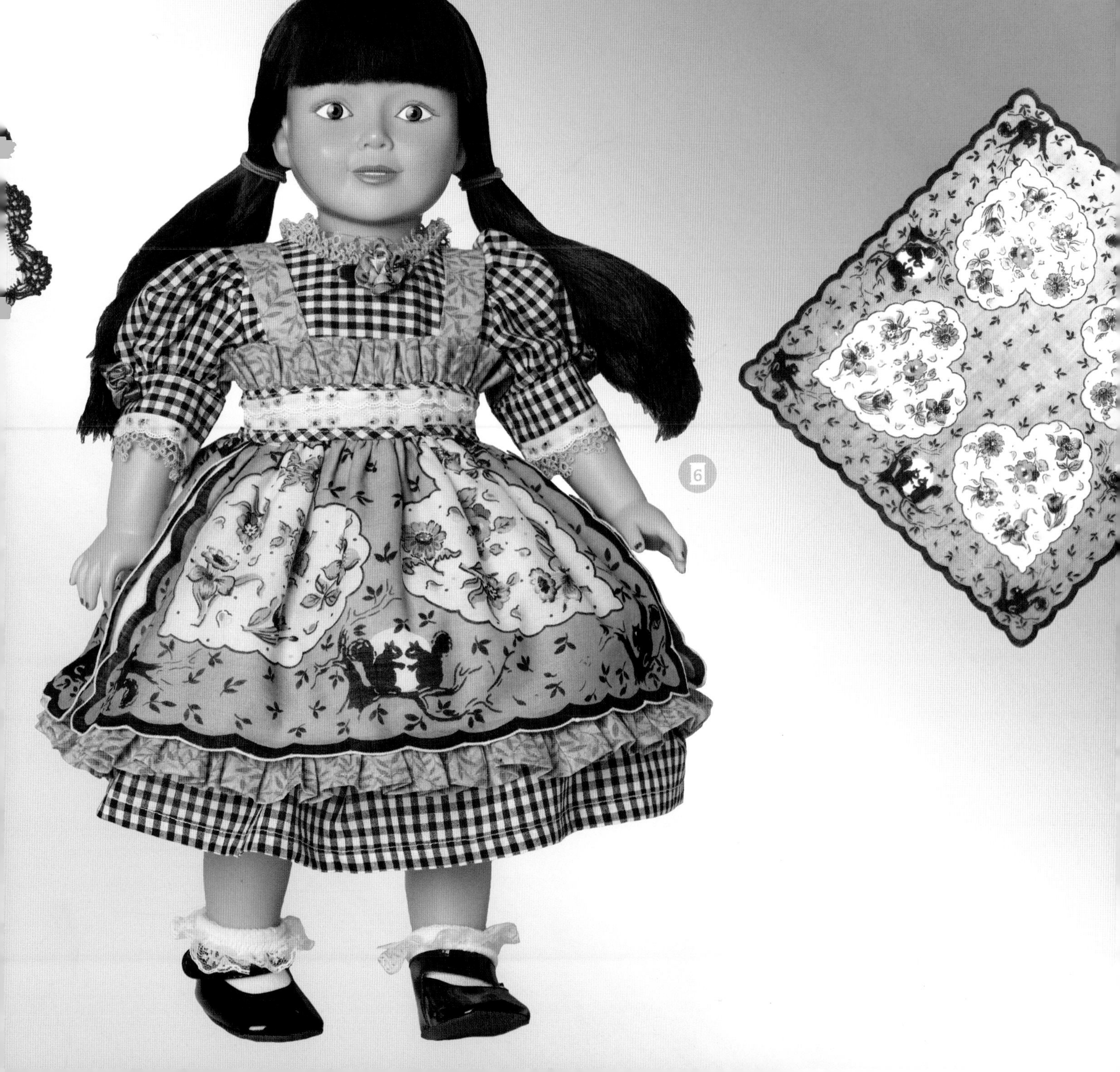

6

Hankie Couture girls love to be

dramatic and colorful.

4

Hankie Couture girls believe that there's a place for everything, and everything has its place. Life is much easier when you're *organized.*

The Hankie Couture Doctrine

depends on these three things:

Details, Details, Details!

Clef perdue
la clef de mon coeur
N'oubliez pas vos clefs
Do not forget your keys

Hankie Couture's view
of the world: life's
idiosyncrasies
are so amusing!

Hankie Couture Little Known Fact:

Optimism

is her secret weapon!

4

5

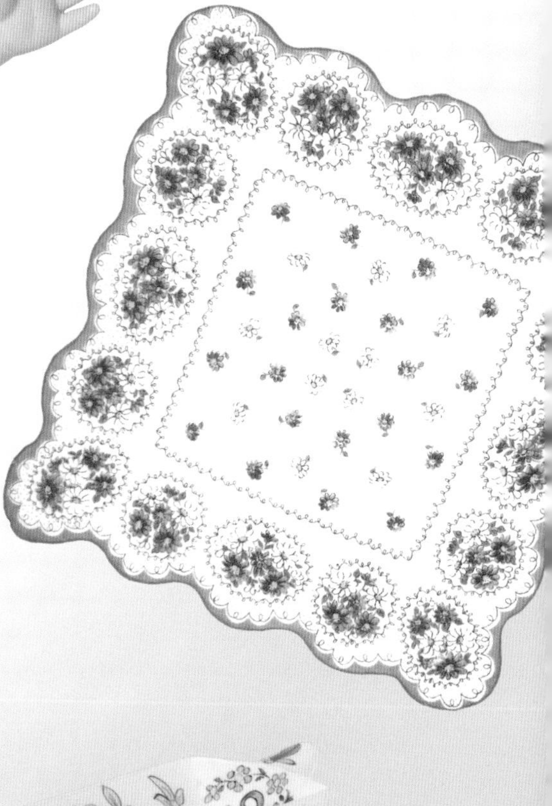

Boldness is contagious!
Hankie Couture girls
are full of
exuberant ideas!

The young ladies of Hankie
Couture love to visit
antique stores, flea markets,
and swap meets to find the
perfect hankie
to create a new dress!

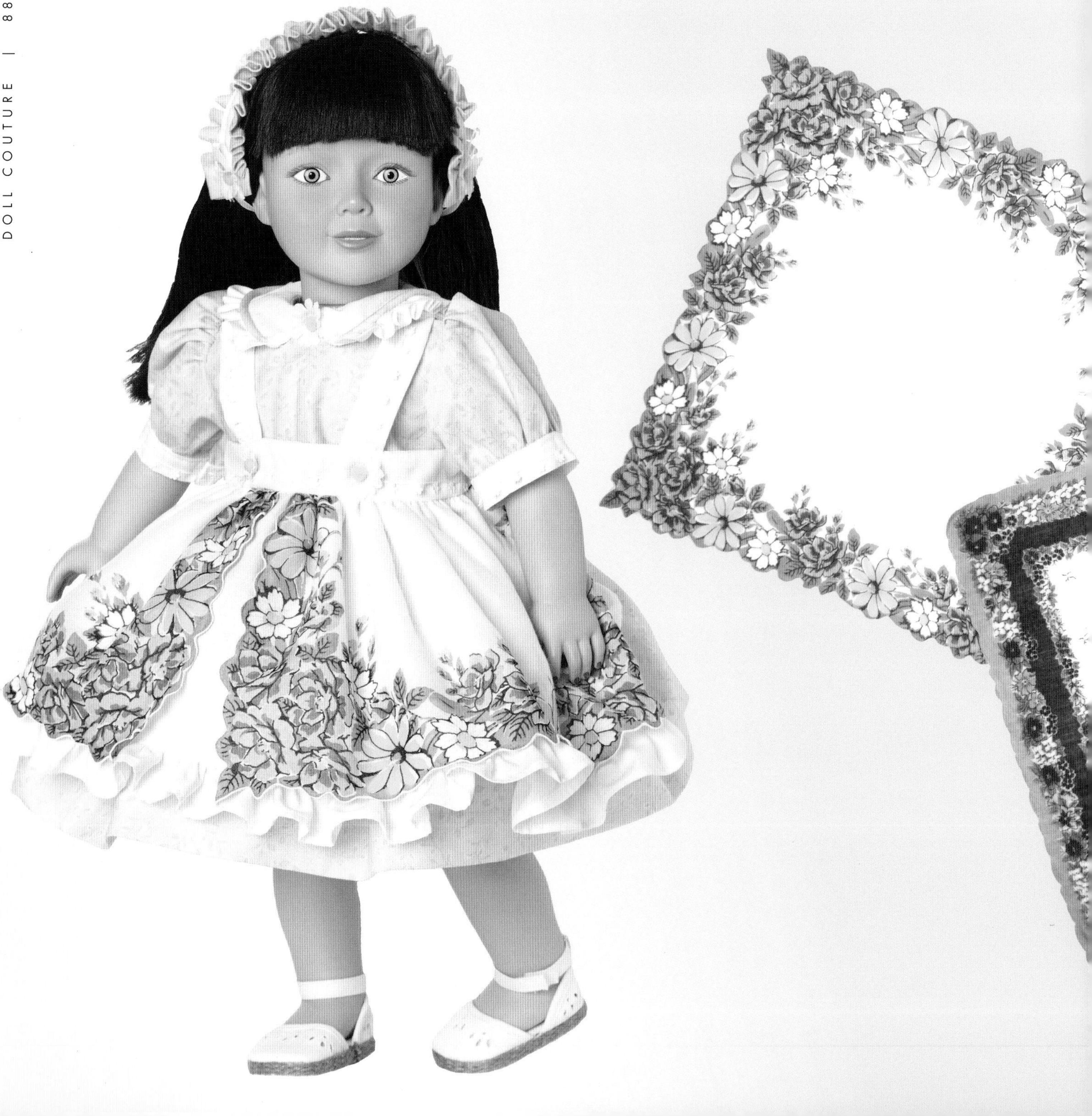

Charm and *cheerfulness* are only two of a Hankie Couture girl's assets!

6

Hankie Couture
girls know that
smiling brings
people into your world.

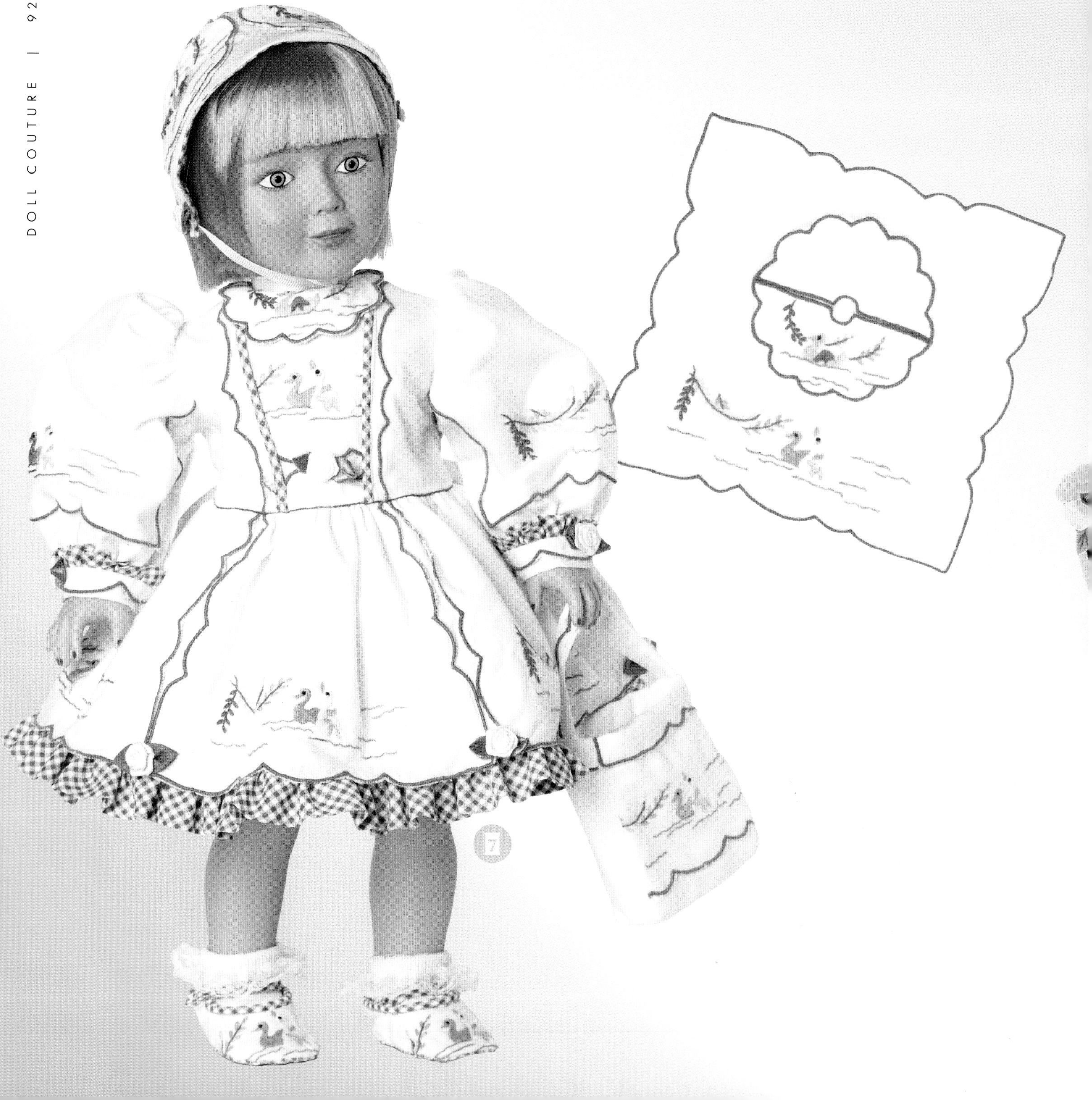
7

Hankie Couture girls feel a

heartfelt connection

to nature.

For a Hankie Couture girl,
every act of high
achievement begins with
creative freedom.

Ah! The art of the dance!
H.C. girls know the importance of
comfort and ease
of movement.

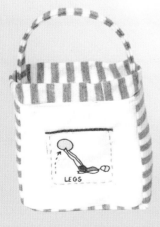

Simple Hankie Couture arithmetic:

Make every day count!

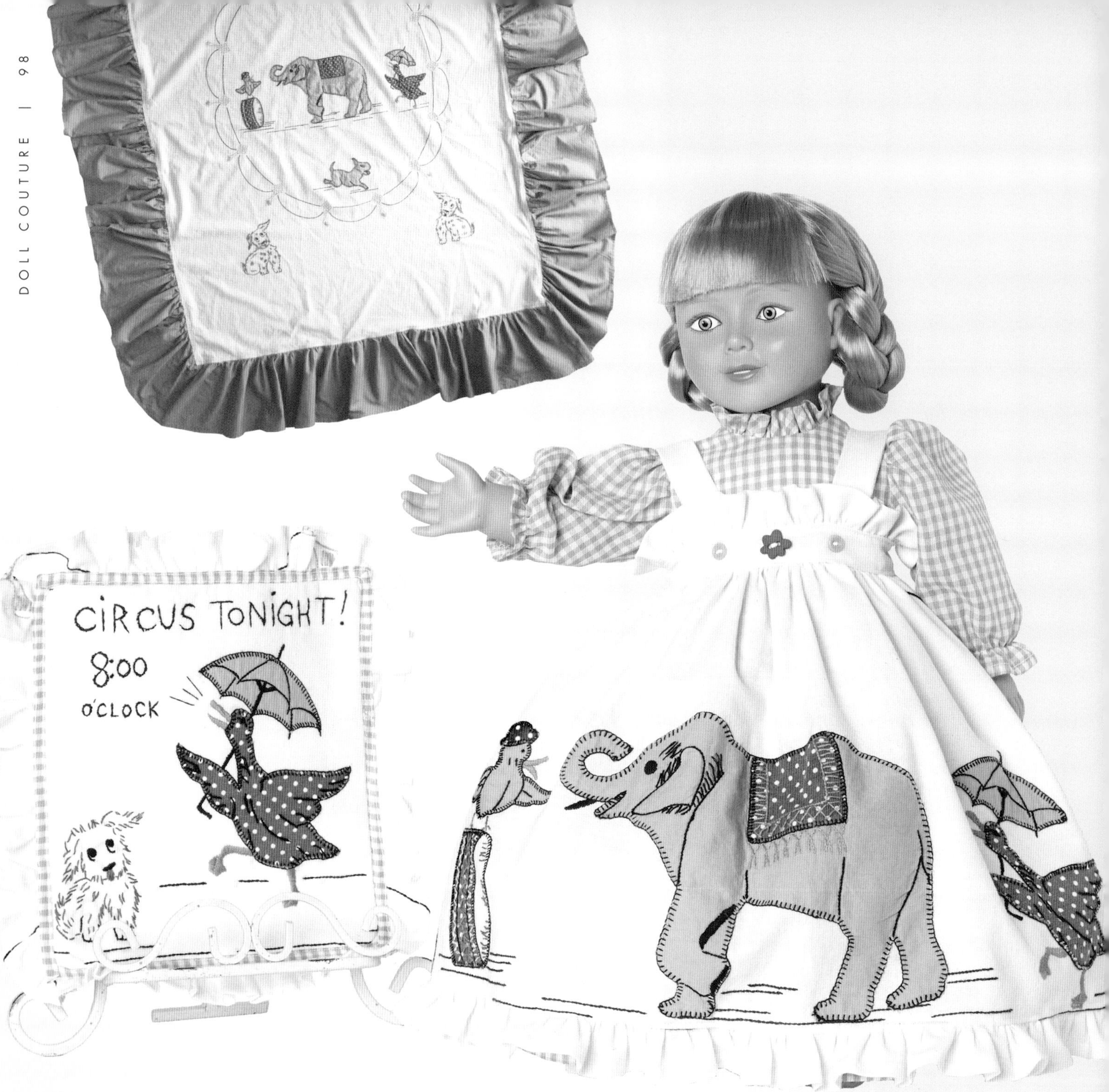
CIRCUS TONIGHT!
8:00
O'CLOCK

Hankie Couture
girls like the sense of
adventure spent on a
*"creative
rampage!"*

When it comes to charisma,
Hankie Couture girls are
completely original.
It's in their DNA!

A Hankie Couture truism: Being

surrounded by loved ones is

heaven on earth.

The breath of her dreams,
her perfect grace,
her confidence:
These are attributes that
come naturally to a
Hankie Couture girl.

A Hankie Couture girl is full of delightful surprises! She enjoys her perch in the spotlight and prefers to let her *imagination* and intuition run wild!

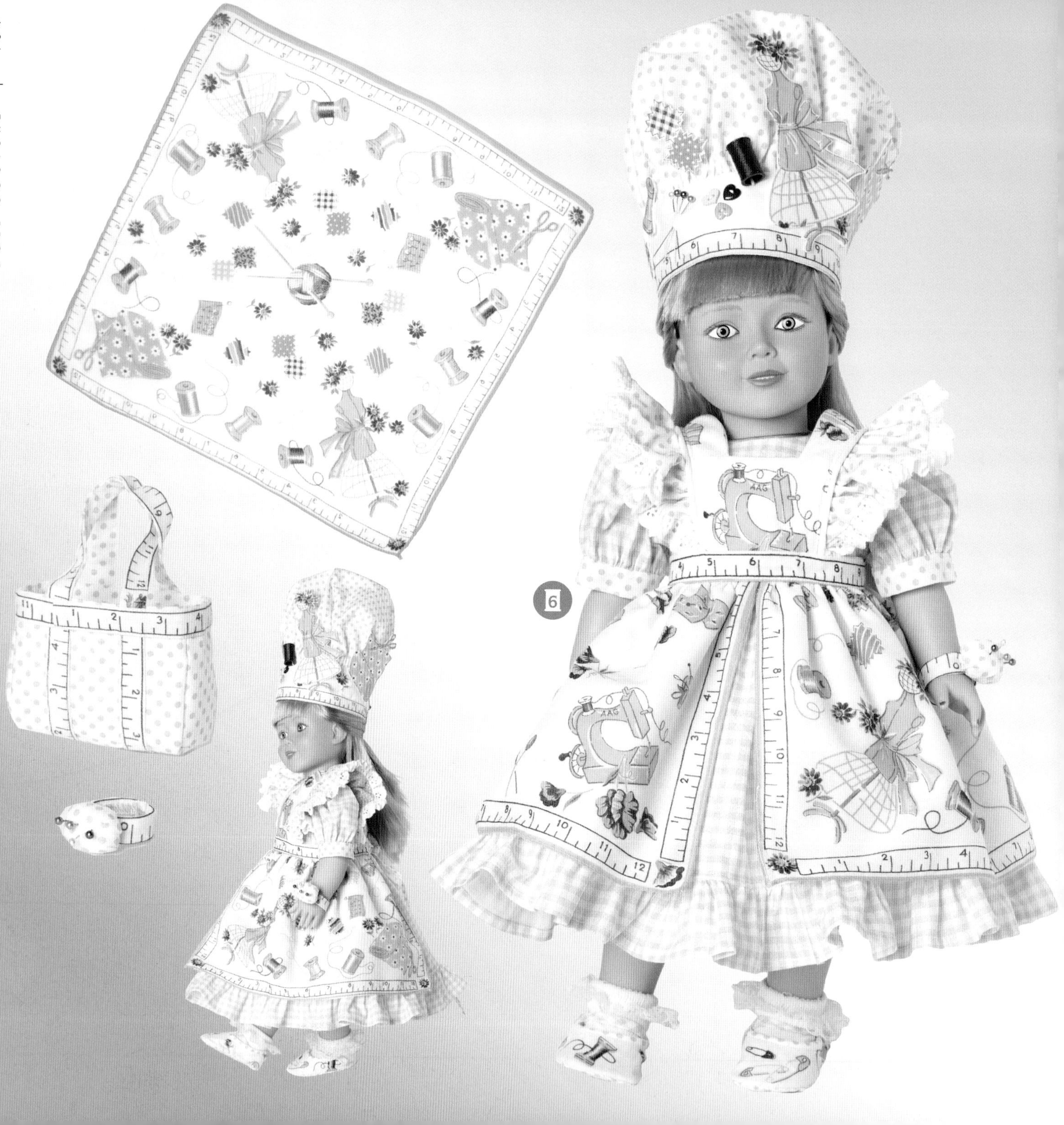
6

The daughters of Hankie Couture
fancy vintage clothing with a
distinctive edge.
Social rules here dictate
the love of the hat and all
its embellishments.

Hankie Couture girls
realize the importance
and power of the
imagination.

6

A Hankie Couture girl
knows that writing a
heartfelt note
makes a most
memorable gift.

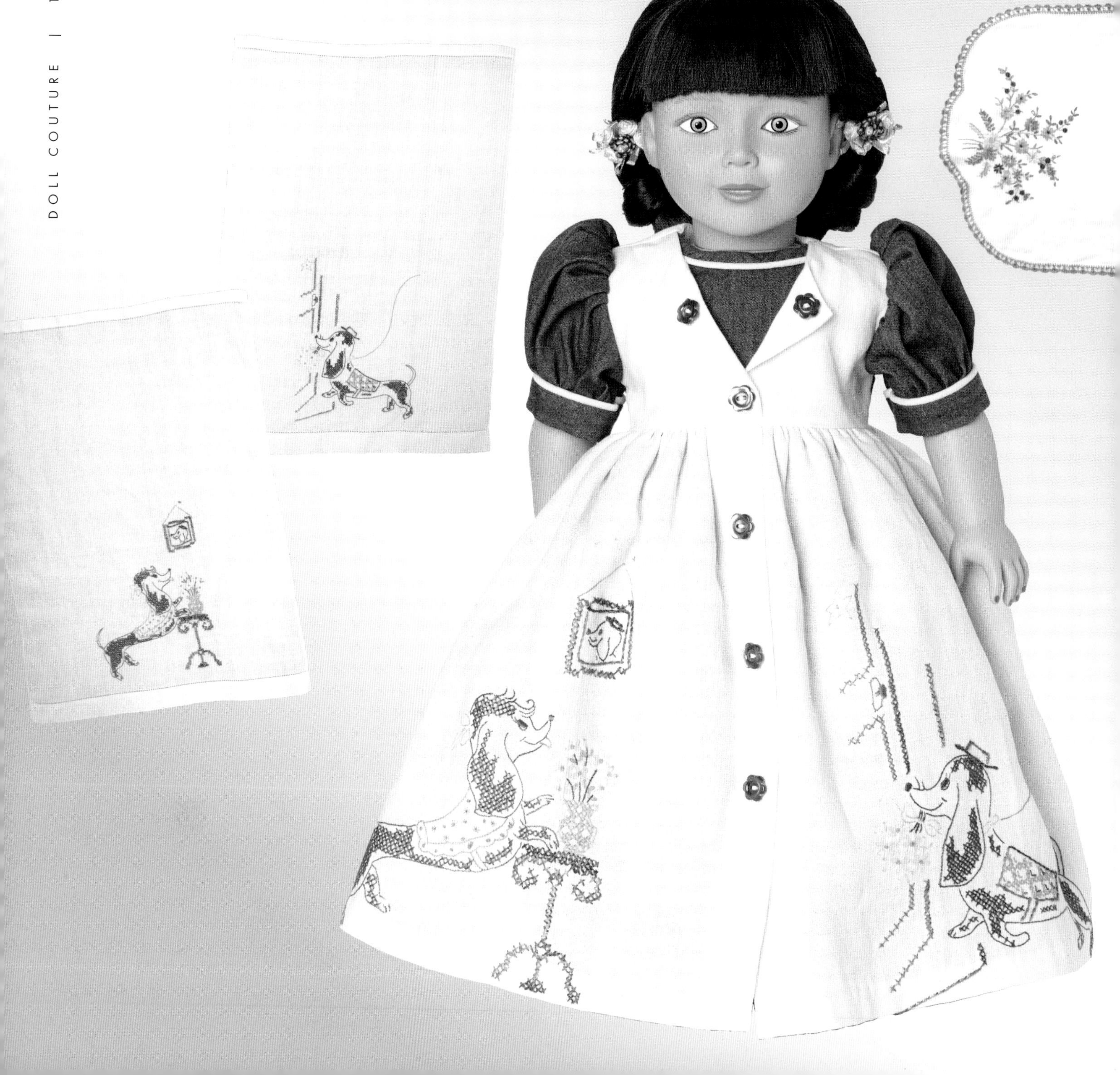

Hankie Couture: Where
*persistence
and
determination*
share center stage.

Combing through *vintage fabrics* brings a wonderful sense of the new.

Hankie Couture girls start
the day with a positive
drive: They pack up their
potential
and head for the fast lane!

Hankie Couture girls
know that learning is
never a straight line.
Success
is just around the corner.

Tis' always the season

in the world of Hankie Couture!

Oh, happy day!

Hankie Couture girls see the

sweetness in everyone.

What a *delicious* day!
I could eat it with a spoon!

6

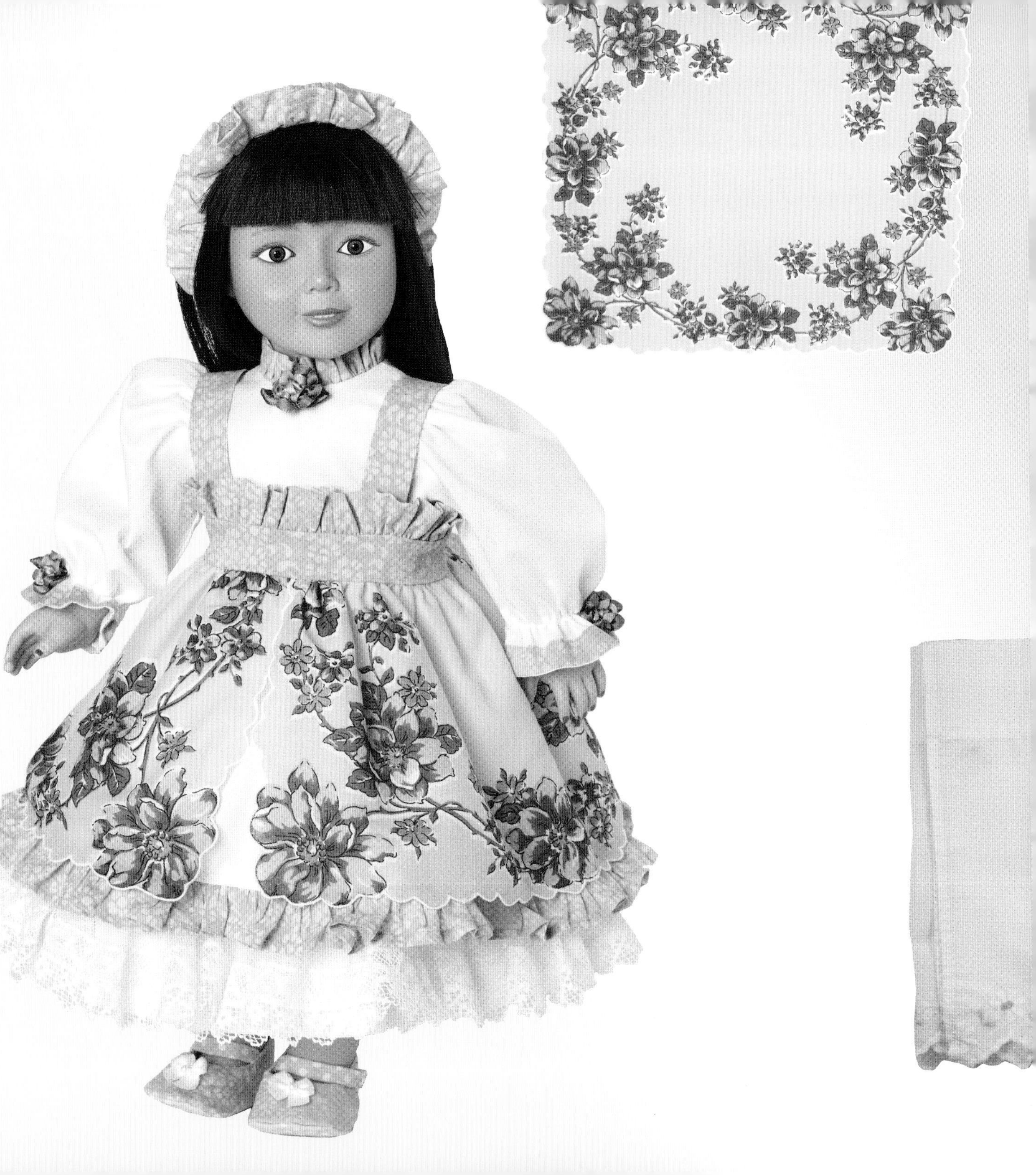

The girls of Hankie Couture
have a natural spontaneity
and sophistication of thought.
They are as refreshing as
sunshine!

Hankie Couture girls
find it easy to be gracious
and treat everyone with
respect.

Warm
puppies
are nice!

How Hankie Couture girls

enhance their creativity:

1. Go for a brisk walk.

2. Take a hot bubble bath.

3. Eat a big bowl of ice cream!

H.C. girls love to eat.
They are aware that breakfast is the
perfect beginning
to their busy day.

Hankie Couture girls cherish
their friendships.
They bask in the sweet sunshine
of affability and camaraderie.

The girls in the world of Hankie Couture
know that being in control is the
key to greatness.
They focus their behavior on
speaking kindly and keeping positive
attitudes and thoughts.

4
5

Hankie Couture:
Her dresses represent
a rare and
perfect union:
Vintage Couture.

The daughters of Hankie
Couture like to be their
B.E.S.T:
Beautiful. Energetic.
Smart. Truthful.

The young ladies of Hankie
Couture know that
every kind deed
is a step towards becoming
a kind person.

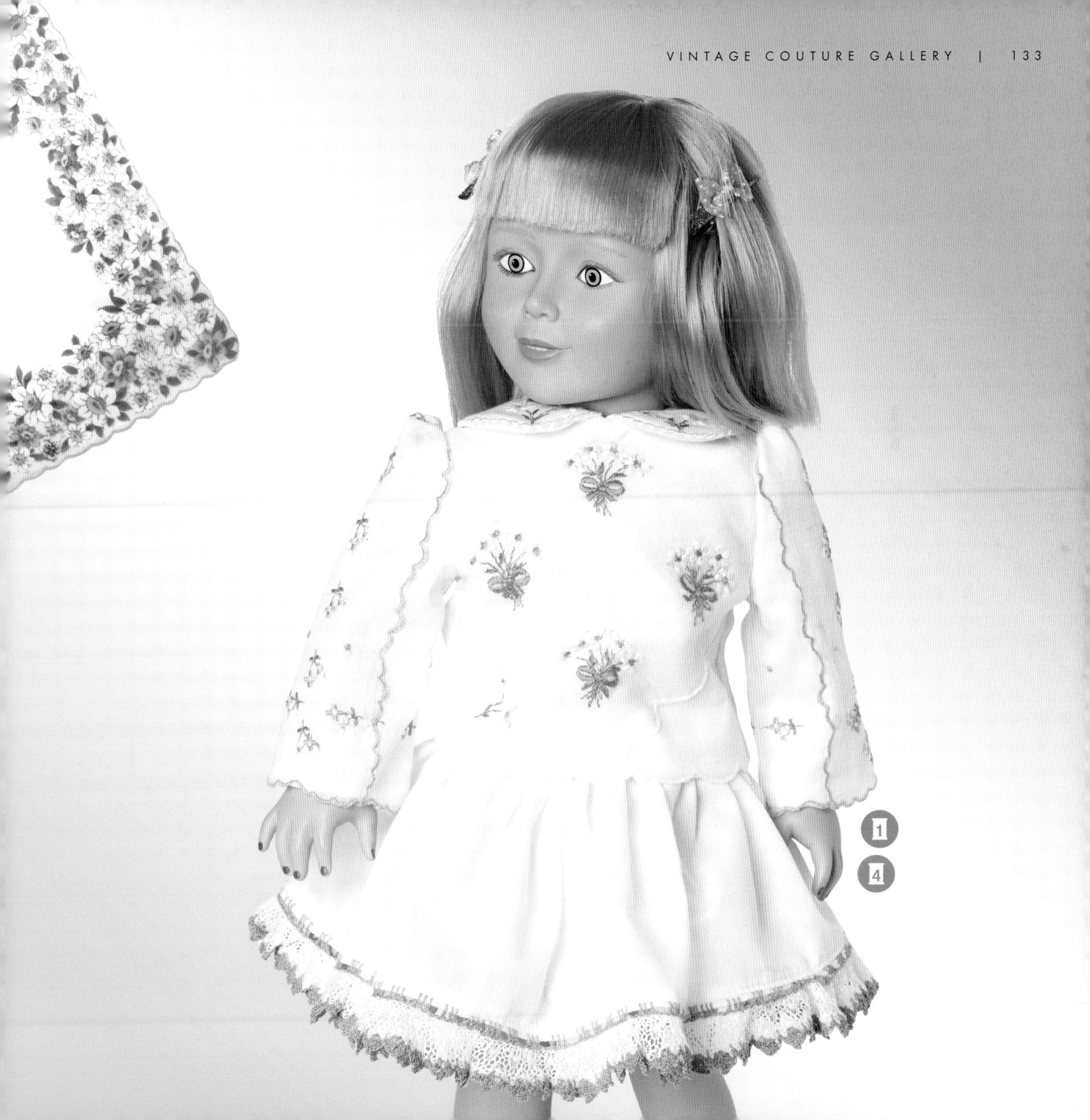
1
4

The sweet girls of Hankie Couture like
to bring joy to others.
They speak with love and concern . . .
and a smile!

General Sewing Instructions

I highly recommend reading all the instructions several times before you begin sewing to familiarize yourself with all the steps. The instructions may not seem 100% clear at first, but repeated readings of the instructions will make things easier for when you actually sit down to sew.

Before cutting into your vintage hankie, tablecloth, pillowcase, take a moment to study it. Get to know it. If there are any flaws, mark them so that area can be cut around or used in the back where it would not show. Remember to cut out the largest pieces first, such as the skirt and sleeves, then cut the smaller pieces like the front/back bodices, collars and cuffs. Lay the pattern pieces over the fabrics where you think the design looks best. Don't hesitate to move the pattern pieces around until it feels right and looks good.

I tried to include "something for everyone". It helps to have a basic knowledge of sewing and many of the styles are simple enough for a beginner. A newcomer can start with the Sleeveless Dress with the Band border and eventually move on to the "Pin Tucked Bodice dress", which has a higher degree of difficulty. Of course, a more advanced sewer can add her/his own touches.

Hankie dresses can require several hankies just for the bodice! The front and back of the bodice can use one full hankie. The sleeves can use another full hankie. If you decide to make long sleeves, you will need two hankies, one for each sleeve! I used nine different embroidered hankies for one hankie dress (see the dress with the house embroidered on the front bodice!).

1   Always try the garment on your doll for a proper fit, *especially before you make the buttonholes or add snaps.*

2   When attaching the bodice to the skirt, make a point to check the front to see that the center of the bodice front matches the center front of the skirt.

3   Press as you go! Press each step along the way! Sewing is only half the work: pressing makes your garment look finished.

4   When buying contrasting fabric, buy at least one yard per dress. This will allow you the option to include shoes and/or a hat and purse. Also, if you see a secondary fabric that "twin's" nicely with your hankie, buy at least ¼ yard. This can be used for cuffs, collar, waistband or spaghetti tie.

5   All seams are ¼" unless otherwise noted. Usually, I allow ½" back seam for the skirt or dress.

6   **Important information when using vintage pieces with finished edges:** Many of my dresses are made using the *original* finished edge, scalloped edge or hand rolled edge of a hankie, tablecloth or pillowcase, tea towel, etc. In these instances, no hem is required.

7   When using the original finished or hand-rolled edge as your hem, *turn up the hem on the pattern piece,* then place the pattern piece along the *finished edge of the vintage hankie, tablecloth, pillow case, tea towel, etc.*

8   **Important:** *When using a scalloped edge as your hem,* place the bottom of the pattern at the tip (or lowest point) of the *deepest scallop.*

9   **The patterns can be intermixed!** For instance, if you want to make the Sleeveless Dress with Contrast Band Border, you can substitute the sleeveless bodice for a bodice with sleeves. Or, you can substitute a short sleeve bodice with cuff to a long sleeve without a cuff (example: Inset Bodice Sleeve).

10 Please refer to the dresses in the book for ideas!

Materials:

⅜" buttons

Laces

Piping

Satin flowers

Pearls

Snaps

Antique jewelry

Sewing Instructions for Clothes Patterns

SKIRT

There are three different lengths on this pattern: short (knee length) medium (midcalf) and long (ankle).

I have allowed hem allowances for all three lengths, however, if you will be using the finished edge or scalloped edge of a table runner, tablecloth or pillowcase, etc, as the *finished edge for the hem*, first *turn up the hem allowance on the pattern piece.* Now place the pattern on the *raw edge* of the vintage fabric or on the scalloped edge. *Important: Place the bottom of the pattern at the tip of the deepest scallop.*

When using the edge of a vintage hankie as your finished edge, cut the hankie in half and place side edges next to each other. Use a white or colored lining fabric as the "underneath" part of the skirt and place the two hankie halves in the center of the lining fabric or leave a space in between the two halves of the hankies. The space in between the two halves can be 1 to 4 inches. The larger the space in between the two hankie halves, the more lining will show. (See photos in this book to find many examples of this concept!) The lining fabric will be showing on each side. This is fine!

If desired, you can "twin" a second hankie to the skirt to take up some of the white lining. Since this extra white lining fabric will be showing in the back of the skirt anyway, adding a second hankie is purely optional.

This skirt style is very full. If you have a beautiful vintage piece of fabric you want to use for the skirt and you do not have enough of the fabric, you can easily reduce the fullness of the skirt by omitting 8 to 10 inches. The skirt will still have plenty of fullness.

Instructions for Skirt with Hem:

1   Follow steps 1–13.

2   Over-lock raw edge of hem.

3   Turn up hem allowance.

4   Machine stitch or blind stitch hem in place.

5   Enjoy your pretty skirt!

Instructions for Skirt with Scalloped or Finished Edge:

1. Gather the upper edges of the skirt with two rows of gathering stitches between small dots.

2. Press under ¼" on one long edge and short ends of the waistband.

3. Over-lock or zigzag center back seam edges of the skirt.

4. Press under ½ "on center back seam edges of the skirt.

5. With right sides together, pin skirt to waistband, matching centers.

6. Pull up gathering stitches to fit on the waistband. Baste.

7. Stitch waistband to skirt.

8. Press seam toward band.

9. Fold band in half, wrong sides together. Pin pressed edge of the waistband over the seam.

10. Hand stitch pressed edge over the seam and across the ends.

11. Try the skirt on your doll for proper fit.

12. Overlap the left back of the band over the right band.

13. Fasten with two snaps.

Pattern

(found in back pocket of book)

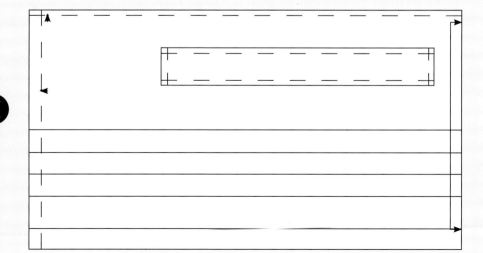

DRESS WITH CONTRAST BAND BORDER

This set of instructions for this dress is for a sleeveless style; however, the *bodice pattern (with sleeves)* for the Dress with Round or Pointed Collar, can be used for this style by substituting steps 1–17 (from those styles) for Steps 1–7 (from this style).

Instructions:

1. **Sleeveless Bodice:** With right sides together, sew the bodice backs to bodice front together at the shoulders. Press seam open.

2. **Bodice lining:** Repeat step 1.

3. **Sewing bodice to lining:** With right sides together, pin the bodice lining to the bodice, matching shoulder seams. Starting at the lower back, stitch one back seam, then stitch the other back seam.

4. Stitch around neck edge and around armholes. Clip neck edges and around armholes, *then* trim the seams slightly.

5. Turn right side out. Press.

6. **Sewing side seams:** Open out the bodice front and backs. With right sides together, pin the bodice front lining to the bodice back lining at the sides. *Stitch in one continuous seam.* Turn, pressing seams toward the back.

7. Repeat with other side.

8. **Skirt:** If using a hankie, cut hankie in half.

9. Open out skirt lining. Mark center with a pin.

10. Place *wrong* sides of the "half hankies" to *right* side of skirt lining, placing the short edge of the "half hankies" in the center next to the pin. The two edges of the hankies will be touching.

11. OPTIONAL: If desired, you can leave a little space in between the two hankie halves. In this case, place each "half hankie" 1" or 2" from the *center front* of the lining. **Please note:** There will be lining fabric showing to the *right* and *left* of the hankie sections. The lining will be at the back of the dress.

12. Gather upper edge of the skirt with two rows of gathering stitches.

13. **Band border:** With wrong sides together, fold band piece in half lengthwise. Press.

14. With right sides together, stitch band to skirt lining. Stitch. Overlock or zigzag seam. Press seam toward skirt lining.

15. Top stitch along seam about ⅛" from edge.

16. Overlock or zigzag side edges.

17   Press under ½" on each side.

18   **Attaching skirt to bodice:** Mark the center of the skirt with a straight pin. Pin center of skirt to the center of the bodice, matching back opening edges of the skirt with the back edge of the bodice.

19   Pull up gathering stitches of skirt. Adjust gathers. Stitch. Overlock seam. Press seam toward bodice. Edge stitch bodice along seam about ⅛" from edge.

20   With right sides together, stitch center back seam, ending about 4" from the bottom of the skirt.

21   **Buttonholes and Buttons:** Mark and sew button holes to bodice left back. Sew buttons to bodice right back.

22   Press dress. Add flowers or other embellishments, if desired.

23   Enjoy your unique and lovely creation!

Pattern

(found in back pocket of book)

CIRCULAR CROCHET DRESS/CIRCULAR SKIRT

The first step is that I highly recommend reading all the instructions before you begin cutting or sewing to familiarize yourself with the construction!

Most of the crochet dresses that I designed for this book were made from two circular crochet doilies. The underneath doily or "lining doily" gives the skirt extra dimension and fullness. Many size doilies can be used for the skirt portion of the dress. Start with at least a 16" doily and you can go up to a 28" doily. It is not necessary to use two doilies for a dress; however, whether you use one or two doilies, the dress *will still* need to be lined.

The circular skirt pattern includes a "guide" pattern piece (which represents the approximate circumference of the waistline) that is cut out and placed on the center of the doily. Please treat the guide piece as just that: a guide. It is entirely possible that the waistline area may need to be enlarged. This is easily done by trimming away ¼" around the waist until the skirt fits easily over the doll's hips.

Please keep in mind to use a doily that is not too thick. This is especially true if you are using two doilies to complete your dress. If you are not using the second "lining doily," just proceed with the instructions and omit the "lining doily." Please remember *not* to cut the doily until it is pinned to the lining fabric!

Remember this if you are using two doilies: As a rule, whatever size doily you choose for the top doily, the underneath "lining doily" needs to be at least 2" longer.

I find that a doily with "ruffles" on the bottom makes a lovely lining doily for your dress!

The rule here is, the smaller the doily, the shorter the skirt. The larger the doily, the longer the skirt. For a knee-length skirt, use a 16" or 18" doily. For a floor-length skirt, use a 24", 26", or larger doily.

In general, I have included two methods of cutting out a circular crochet doily skirt.

First method: Use the pattern guide I have provided.

Second method: Use a seam gauge or tape measurer.

"Seam Gauge Method" for a knee-length skirt: Have handy a 6" seam gauge or tape measure. From the bottom of the doily, measure up 6" all the way around the bottom of the circular doily. Mark the 6" with pins.

Floor-length skirt: Use a large doily: 24" or 26". Measure from the bottom of the doily up 9–10" all the way around. Mark the 9" or 10" with pins.

If you wish to use a large 24" doily but you don't want to make a floor-length skirt, you can still make a short skirt from this larger size doily. In this case, use the "Seam Gauge Method" of measuring your skirt. The waistline will be very big and there will be fullness at the waist.

Important tip: The bigger the center of the doily that gets cut out, the more gathers there will be on the skirt. This also affects the length of the skirt.

Save the center part of the doily that gets cut out as it can be used later to make a matching hat or purse!

Materials:

One 16" diameter or larger doily. This is the "main" doily that will become the skirt.

One doily with a *ruffled* edge for underneath (optional). This is the secondary doily, which will serve as a "lining doily" to the main doily. This second doily should be at least 2" larger than the main doily so that it will show underneath.

One yard of 45-inch wide fabric for the under lining of the skirt. This may be more than you need, but it is always better to have more yardage than not enough. (If you choose to line the skirt with a contrast color, test out how it looks before cutting.)

18" of ⅜-inch wide ribbon for waistline "belt" or cut spaghetti pattern for thin belt

2 or 3 buttons, ⅜"

Instructions:

The following directions are for using two doilies. If you are using only one doily, just omit the lining doily.

1   Wash and dry your doily in the dryer, don't air dry. Press well, stretching the doily as you go around the entire piece.

2   Open out the lining fabric and place the "lining doily" on the fabric, leaving at least 2" all around the *outer* edge.

3   Place the "main" doily over the "lining" doily, matching the centers.

4   Spread out both doilies with your fingers, stretching slightly.

5   Center the *inner circle pattern guide* over the doilies having the center "dot" on the guide directly over the center of the doily. Pin pattern to doily.

6   Now, place pins just to the right of the pattern guide going around the circle, pinning through all the thicknesses. It's okay to have the pins touching each other. Be sure to pin through three layers (if you are using the two doilies). Remove pattern guide piece.

7 **Cutting out the fabric lining:** Cut the lining at least *2" longer than the longest doily.* If your doily has a scalloped edge, follow the scallops OR cut a straight line, but be sure to cut 2" *longer* than the doily.

8 Take the doilies (that are pinned to the white lining) to the sewing machine and stitch around the inner waistline with a wide zigzag stitch, *removing the pins as you go.* Use the pins as your guide. You are stitching through two doilies and the white lining, so it will be slightly thick.

9 Stitch around the inner waistline one more time.

10 Press the waistline edge.

11 **Waistline:** Cut out the crochet doily (or doilies) as close to the zigzag stitching as possible. Cut slowly with small scissors. **Do not cut the white lining!**

12 Cut the lining in the center a generous ⅜" larger than the doily. (You will be using the ⅜" lining to attach the skirt to the bodice as the doilies are too bulky to sew directly to the bodice.) Save the center section of the crochet doily to be used for a hat or a purse.

13 **Back Center Seam:** Now you will be creating a back center seam. Look carefully at your doily. If you see any part of the doily with a slight flaw, use that part of the doily for the "center back seam" of the skirt.

14 Thread a needle with a contrasting thread. To determine where the center back seam will be, run a basting stitch at the "center back" down from the waistline to about 3 ½".

15 Zigzag to the left and right of the basting thread. Remove the basting thread.

16 *Carefully* cut through all the thicknesses in between the two rows of zigzag stitching.

17 Run two rows of gathering stitching around the waistline. The first row should be ¼" from the raw edge, the second row ⅛" from the raw edge.

18 Turn under ¼" on center back seam edges. Press.

19 At the bottom of the back seam edge, with right sides together, stitch a small dart about 1 ½" long. This will help the bottom of the center back seam to lie flat. Look at the right side of the skirt at the back seam and check to make sure it is lying flat. Press well!

20 Now you are ready to sew the crochet doily skirt to the bodice. Prepare the bodice following the instructions for the **bodice of your choice:** short sleeve, long sleeve, inset bodice, etc.

21 **Sewing the bodice to the crochet doily skirt:** with right sides together, pin the center of the bodice to the center of the skirt white lining, not actually to the crochet doilies themselves.

22   Pin bodice back to center back seam of the skirt. Adjust the crochet skirt to fit to the bodice. Pin. Baste. **Special note:** Depending on the size of your doily, there may not be much to gather into the bodice. This is fine as the skirt will lie flat at the waist and be full at the bottom!

23   Look at the front of the crochet dress. You should have captured all of the white lining in the seam allowance. If not, go back and stitch closer! Stitch again over same stitching. Over lock raw edge.

24   Press seam toward bodice.

25   Edge stitch ⅛" from seam on bodice.

26   Place a ⅜" ribbon over the waistline. (If you see some zigzag stitches, this is okay as the ribbon should cover it up). Hand-stitch or machine stitch in place.

27   **Adjusting the white lining on the skirt:** Try the dress on your doll. The white lining will be hanging lower than the crochet doily skirt.

28   I recommend cutting the lining while on the doll, so at this point, you have several choices. If you like the lining peeking out from underneath the crochet doily skirt, just make a small hem. If the lining looks too long, measure out how much you want to trim and cut the lining carefully and slowly, then hem. If the doily has a scalloped edge, carefully cut the lining to follow the scalloped edge. Zigzag the raw edge.

29   **Buttonholes and Buttons:** Make 2 or 3 buttonholes at bodice left back. Sew buttons to bodice right back.

Now, back to the little center section of the doily! The center can be used for a hat or purse.

Pattern

(found in back pocket of book)

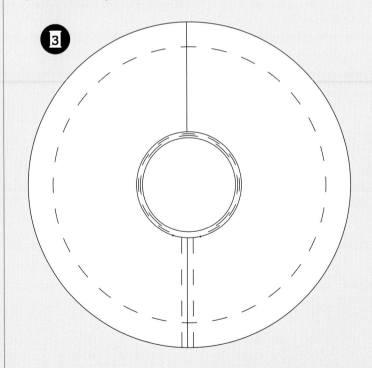

HAT OR PURSE

Materials:

20" of 1/4" ribbon for hat ties

8" of 1/4" ribbon for purse

3/4" of 1" ruffled lace, to go around the hat or purse
(measure the diameter to determine how much lace to buy)

Seam Gauge or Tape Measure

Instructions for Crochet Hat:

1. Place the crochet center section over a small piece of lining. Pin in place. Zigzag around the entire edge. Trim the lining close to the stitching.

2. Thread a needle and stitch around the outside edge, pulling up on the doily until you achieve the desired "roundness." Try the hat on the doll. Adjust gathers, then secure a tight knot.

3. Add ½" trim or lace to edge if desired.

4. Cut two ribbons each 10" long. Sew one tie to each side.

Instructions for Crochet Purse:

1. Place crochet center section over a small piece of lining. Pin in place. Zigzag around entire edge. Trim lining close to the zigzag stitching.

2. Sew ruffled lace around the edge of the doily. Sew the center of the lace to the edge so that half the lace will be on the doily and the other half of the lace will hang just over the edge of the doily.

3. Fold doily in half.

4. Tack the side edges together so the "purse" stays closed. It is not necessary to close the purse all the way. You just don't want it flopping open.

5. Pin the ribbon handle to each side of the purse. Try the purse on the doll to see just how long you would like the handle to be. Sew ribbon "handle" to the inside of the lining on each side of the purse.

BLOUSE

Instructions:

1 **Bodice:** With right sides together, stitch the bodice backs to bodice front together at the shoulders. Press seams open.

2 Stay stitch ¼" around neck edge.

3 **Collar:** Fuse interfacing to two collar sections.

4 **Piping (optional):** Pin piping along the outer edge of both collar sections, placing the edge of the piping even with the edge of the collar. You will need to clip the corners. Baste in place.

5 With right sides together, pin the collar lining sections to the collar sections with the piping. Using a zipper foot, stitch the collar sections together, leaving the neck edge open. Sew as close as possible to the ridge of the piping. Trim seam to ⅛". Turn right side out. Press. Check your work! If you did not sew close enough to the piping the first time, go back and stitch closer. Baste the raw edges together.

6 Lightly tack the front collar sections together by overlapping front sections a scant ¼".

7 Place the wrong side of the collar to the right side of the blouse, having the center of the collar matched to the center of the blouse. Clip the neck edge as necessary. Baste in place.

8 **Bodice lining:** With right sides together, stitch the bodice backs to bodice front together at the shoulders.

9 **Sewing blouse to blouse lining:** With right sides together, pin the blouse lining to the blouse matching the shoulder seams. Starting at the lower back, stitch one back seam, then stitch the other back seam.

10 Stitch around the neck edge. The curved edge around the neck line needs to be clipped so that the bodice can be turned inside out and lie flat. Carefully clip the neckline at ¼" intervals, being very careful not to cut past the stitching line. Trim seam slightly. Turn. Press.

11 **Sleeves:** Gather the upper and lower edge of sleeve with two rows of gathering stitches between small dots.

12 **Sleeve Bands:** Fuse interfacing to band sections.

13 Press under ¼" on long remaining edge of each band.

14 **Attaching sleeves to sleeve band:** With right sides together, pin band to lower edge of sleeves. Pull up threads and adjust gathers to fit. Baste. Stitch. Turn seam allowance toward band.

15 **Attaching sleeves to bodice:** With right sides together, pin sleeve to armhole edges, placing the center notch on the sleeve to the shoulder seam. Adjust the gathers; baste. Stitch. Stitch again ⅛" away in the seam allowance. Lightly press the seam allowances toward sleeve.

16 **Sewing side seams:** With right sides together, pin the bodice front to the bodice backs at sides. Pin underarm sleeve edges together. Stitch in one continuous seam. Overlock raw edges with a zigzag stitch or, if you have an overlock machine, overlock the raw edges.

17 Fold band in half and hand-sew pressed edge over sleeve seam. Press.

18 Press side seams toward back.

19 Overlock or zigzag bottom edge of blouse. Turn up ¼" of hem.

20 **Buttonholes and buttons:** Mark and sew buttonholes to left back. Sew buttons to right back. Be sure to measure the exact placement of the buttons before you sew them onto the blouse! If desired, you may use snaps.

21 Press. Admire your work!

Pattern

(found in back pocket of book)

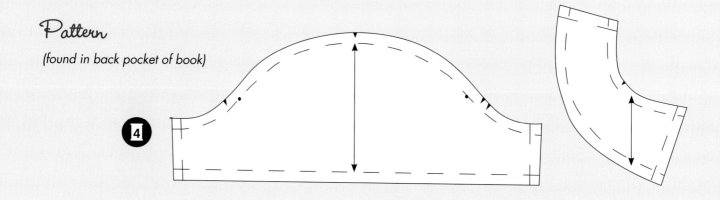

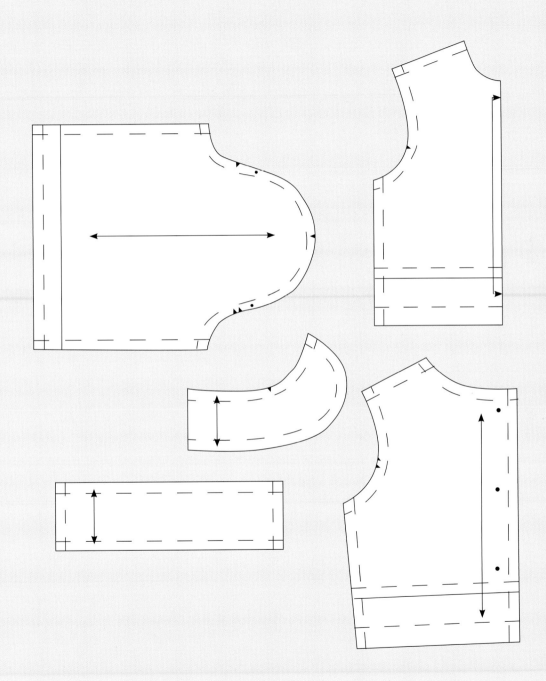

ROMPER

Instructions:

1. With right sides together, stitch center front seam. Clip curves. Press seam to one side.

2. With right sides together, stitch back to front together at side seams. Press seam toward back.

3. Repeat steps 1 and 2 for lining.

4. *Separately* zigzag or overlock center back seam edges of romper and romper lining.

5. Turn up hem on *lining*. Hem on the *romper* will not be necessary if you used the *finished scalloped edge* of your vintage tea towel, hankie, pillowcase, etc. If you did not use the finished edge, turn up hem and stitch.

6. Pin right side of lining to wrong side of romper.

7. Turn under ¼" on back seams *above notch*. Press.

8. Gather the upper edge of the romper with two rows of gathering stitches. Start and end gathering stitches between *small dots*.

9. **Straps:** fold strap in half, right sides together. Stitch. Turn. Press.

10. **Waistband:** Press interfacing to wrong side of waistband.

11. With right sides together, pin the straps to the interfaced waistband section, matching notches. Baste straps in place.

12. With right sides together, pin waistband lining to waistband. Sew across the top and sides of the waistband. Trim seam. Turn. Press. Baste across raw edge.

13. With right sides together, pin the center of the waistband to the center front of the romper. **Helpful Hint:** Mark the center of the waistband with a pin, then match the pin to the center front seam of the romper. Pull up the gathering stitches of the romper to fit the waistband. Pin. Baste. Sew. Press seam toward waistband. Top stitch ⅛" from seam.

14. **Center back seam of romper:** With right sides together, stitch center back seam to notch.

15. **Center back seam of romper lining:** With right sides together, stitch center back seam to notch.

16. Now you will be sewing the inside leg edges together (separately from the lining). With right sides together, stitch the front to the back at inside leg edges, matching center front and back seams.

17. Repeat Step 15 with the lining.

18 Turn inside out. Fit romper to doll. Sew snaps at back.

19 Press. A beautiful garment is only half finished until it is pressed!

20 Add ribbons, flowers, or buttons to the front of the romper, if desired.

21 Admire your vintage creation!

Pattern

(found in back pocket of book)

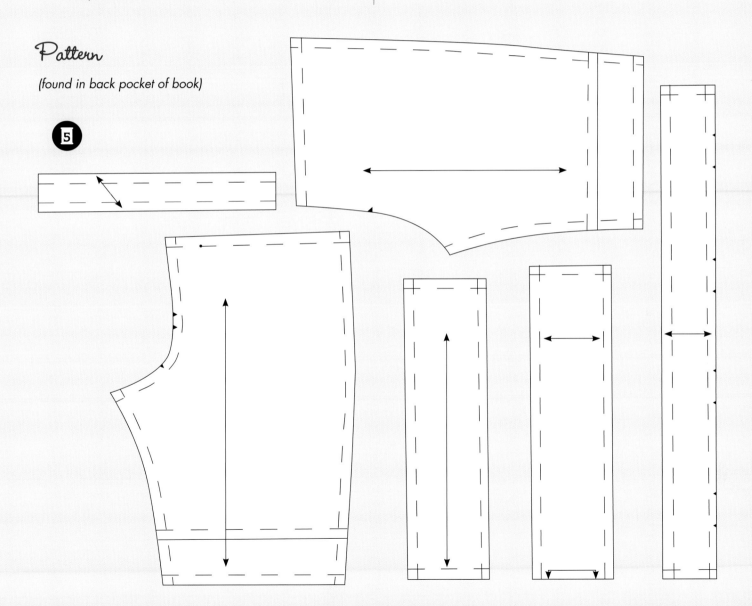

DRESS WITH ROUND OR POINTED COLLAR

Instructions:

1 **Bodice Front:** With right sides together, sew the bodice backs to bodice front together at the shoulders. Press seam open.

2 **Collar:** Fuse interfacing to collar sections.

3 **Piping (optional):** Pin piping along the outer edge of both collar sections, placing the edge of the piping even with the edge of the collar. You will need to clip the corners. Baste.

4 With right sides together, pin the collar lining sections to the collar sections with the piping. Using a zipper foot, stitch the collar sections together, leaving the neck edge open. Sew as close as possible to the ridge of the piping. Trim seam to ⅛". Turn. Press. Baste raw edges together.

5 Lightly tack the front collar sections together, by overlapping front sections a scant ¼".

6 Place the wrong side of the collar to the right side of the bodice, having the center of the collar matched to the center of the bodice. Clip the neck edge as necessary. Baste.

7 **Bodice Lining:** With right sides together, stitch the bodice backs to bodice front together at the shoulders. Press seam open.

8 **Sewing bodice to bodice lining:** With right sides together, pin the bodice lining to the bodice, matching shoulder seams. Starting at the lower back, stitch one back seam, then stitch the other back seam.

9 Stitch around neck edge. Clip neck edges where necessary. Trim seam slightly.

10 Turn right side out. Press, making sure that the collar lies flat.

11 **Sleeves:** Gather the upper and lower edges of the sleeve between the small dots.

12 **Sleeve bands:** Fuse interfacing to two band sections. If you are adding trim or lace, place right side of lace to right side of sleeve band. Baste in place.

13 Stitch interfaced band sections to lining sections along one long edge. Carefully, trim seam to ⅛". Turn. Press. Baste raw edges together.

14 **Attaching sleeve band to sleeve:** With right sides together, pin sleeve band to lower edge of sleeve. Helpful Hint: Mark the center of the lower sleeve edge and center of the sleeve band with a straight pin. Match the pin centers, then draw up the gathering stitches of the sleeve to fit on the sleeve band. Pin as necessary. Stitch. Zigzag or overlock raw edge. Press seam toward sleeve band. Topstitch ⅛" from seam edge on band.

15 **Attaching sleeves to bodice:** With right sides together, pin sleeve to the armhole edge, placing the center notch on the sleeve to the shoulder seam. Adjust the gathers: baste. Stitch. Stitch again ⅛" away in the seam allowance. Lightly press the seam toward the garment.

16 **Sewing side seams:** With right sides together, pin the bodice front to the bodice backs at the sides. Pin underarm sleeve edges together. Stitch in one continuous seam. Overlock raw edges with a zigzag stitch or, use your Overlock machine to overlock the raw edges.

17 Press seam toward back. Tack seam down at sleeve band.

18 **Skirt:** Gather upper edge of skirt with two rows of gathering stitching.

19 Overlock back seams of the skirt. Turn under ½" on each side. Press.

20 Mark the center of the skirt with a straight pin. Pin center of skirt to the center of the bodice, matching back opening edges of the skirt with the back edge of the bodice.

21 Pull up on gathering stitches to fit. Adjust gathers. Stitch. Overlock seam. Press seam toward bodice. Edge stitch bodice along seam, about ⅛" from the edge.

22 With right sides together, stitch center back seam, ending at small notch.

23 **Buttonholes and buttons:** Mark and sew buttonholes to bodice left back. Sew buttons to bodice right back.

24 Press dress. Add flowers or other embellishments, if desired. Enjoy your magnificent creation!

Pattern

(found in back pocket of book)

6

PIN-TUCK INSET BODICE DRESS

This dress can be made without the pintucks. If you wish to substitute an embroidered or solid piece of fabric for the center panel, simply cut it out using the center panel pattern piece.

Helpful Hint on cutting center panel with pintucks: After you have cut the center panel lining piece from the fabric, use this lining piece as your *temporary guide* when cutting out the completed pin-tuck panel. The reason: It "hugs" the fabric and doesn't shift around as much as the tissue pattern.

Pin the center panel lining to the pin-tuck panel using as few pins as possible.

Special information for pin-tucked bodice: If you are using piping, it may be necessary to trim excess fabric from the lining. After step 15, trim the lining slightly to fit the bodice so that they are just about the same size. The reason: the piping ever so *slightly* "shrinks" or pulls up on the fabric, especially around the shoulder area and bottom.

Instructions:

1 **Pin-tuck inset guide piece:** Fuse *featherweight* interfacing to fabric using the guide pattern piece.

2 Mark pin tuck placement with small notches on each side to ensure accuracy.

3 **Making pintucks:** Following guide, fold fabric on solid line. Place the folded edge on the broken line. Stitch. Press pin-tuck down.

4 Make second pin-tuck and all subsequent pin-tucks in the same manner. Note: you may wish to use a contrast stitching for your pintuck pleats. Or, you can match the thread to your fabric. Be sure to press each pin-tuck down *individually* as you go!

5 Using the center front lining piece as your *guide only*, place the center front lining piece over the completed pin-tucked fabric piece, placing the bottom edge of the lining ⅜" from the bottom edge. **Special note:** Make sure the last pin-tuck on the bottom will clear the seam allowance.

6 Pin. Cut out carefully!

7 Stay-stitch the side edges from top to bottom.

8 **Inset bodice without pin-tucks:** Fuse interfacing to front inset bodice piece.

9 **Piping:** Pin piping to bodice front inset at sides. Using a zipper foot, stitch piping to bodice front.

10 With right sides together, pin bodice front to left front bodice and to right front bodice. Stitch. Press seam toward side. Edge stitch close to seam.

11 With right sides together, stitch bodice back and front together at the shoulders. Press seam toward back.

12 Stay-stitch neck edge.

13 Lining: With right sides together, stitch bodice backs to front bodice together at the shoulders. Press seam open.

14 With right sides together, pin the lining to the bodice. Stitch the back seams first, *then* stitch around the neck opening. **Helpful Hint:** I like stitching the back seams first as it "holds" everything in place.

15 Clip around neck edges. *Carefully* trim seams slightly. Turn. Press.

16 **Sleeves:** Gather top of sleeves between notches, using a long machine stitch, stitch ¼" from edge and then ⅛" away within the seam allowance.

17 With right sides together, pin sleeve to armhole, being sure to match the center of the sleeve to the shoulder seam. Pull up the gathering stitches to fit. Baste. Stitch. Overlock raw edges.

18 With right sides together, stitch front to back at entire underarm seams.

19 Skirt: Gather top edge of skirt. To gather, using a long machine stitch, stitch ¼" from edge and then ⅛" away within the seam allowance.

20 Mark the center of the skirt with a straight pin.

21 With right sides together, pin skirt to bodice, matching the center of the bodice to the center of the skirt.

22 Pull up the gathering stitches to fit. Pin. Baste. Before you stitch, turn the dress around and look at it! Make sure the design of the skirt is *centered* to the *center* of the bodice.

23 Stitch. Overlock seam. Gently press seam toward bodice.

24 Top stitch ⅛" from seam.

25 With right sides together, stitch center back seam to small dot.

26 Buttonholes: Make buttonholes on left back. Sew buttons to right back.

27 Enjoy your beautiful, one-of-a-kind creation!

Pattern

(found in back pocket of book)

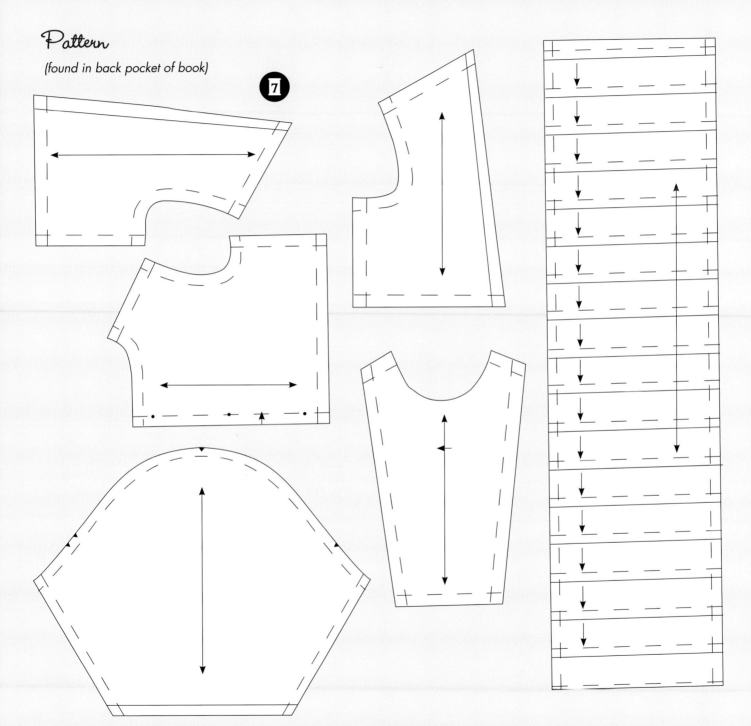

HAT

Materials:

½ yard fabric

Medium-weight interfacing

Flowers (optional)

Ribbons (optional)

Instructions:

1. Fuse interfacing to wrong side of hat brim, hat crown, and hat top.

2. Stitch the center back seam of each brim section.

3. With right sides together, pin the brim section together, matching the centers.

4. Stitch along the outer edge.

5. Turn right side out. Press.

6. Baste the raw edges together.

7. Stitch the center back seam of each crown section.

8. With *wrong* sides together, stitch upper and lower edges of crown sections together.

9. With right sides together, pin hat brim to hat crown, matching the center back seam. Clip where necessary to fit. Stitch.

10. Overlock or zigzag raw edge.

11. Press seam toward crown.

12. With wrong sides together, pin both top hat sections together. Baste around circle.

13. With right sides together, pin top to crown, matching the seams. Clip where necessary.

14. Stitch. Trim seam. Overlock raw edge.

15. Turn right side out. Press.

16. Turn up hat brim.

17. Decorate hat as desired with flowers, ribbons, etc.

Pattern

(found in back pocket of book)

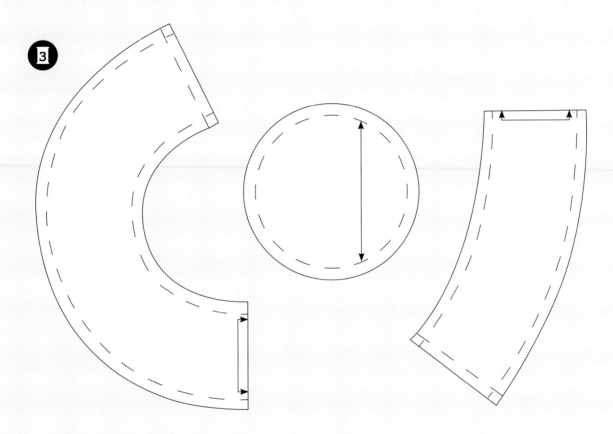

SHOES

When cutting out shoes using embroidered hankies or other embroidered pieces, you will want to have the design, such as a flower centered, to the upper sole. (If your vintage fabric has scalloped edges, so much the better!) You may need to turn the upper sole pattern piece at an angle to be able to have the embroidered flower in the center. If you decide to do this, it may be necessary to piece together the upper shoe piece, as the pattern piece will be "off" the fabric. If you are using fabric with a scalloped edge, lay the scalloped edge over the raw edge of the fabric. If your fabric does not have a scalloped edge, place a piece of trim or narrow lace over the raw edge of the fabric. **Creative Tip:** Your shoes do not have to match! That is part of the fun of creating your own vintage fashions!

If you decide to cut shoes without any embroidery, you can add flowers after you have completed the shoes. I recommend adding flowers *only after* the shoe is completely sewn, to make sure the flowers end up in the center. Try the shoes on the doll to ensure that the flowers end up in the center. Have fun embellishing your shoes with pearls, buttons, and small trinkets. Anything works. Let your creative juices flow!

When cutting the lining, you can use a contrast fabric for the upper shoe, soles, and straps.

These shoes are a little labor-intensive, but that is part of the fun of creating a truly unique pair of shoes to match your dress!

Helpful Hint: Both shoes can be cut at the same time; however, I recommend starting and completely finishing one shoe at a time. There is a right foot sole (cut from cardboard stock) and a left foot sole and you don't want to get them mixed up!

Materials:

Fabric or leftover scraps from the vintage fabric of the dress

Lining—a scrap of fabric is all that is needed

Mid-weight interfacing

Feather-weight interfacing

Snaps: size ⅜

Piping (optional): Use store-bought piping. Or, if you are making your own piping, cut one

15 x 1 ¼" bias strip. (This will be enough for both shoes.)

Small cording to put inside bias strip (15" long)

5 x 5" cardboard square

Elmer's glue

Clothespins (about 16)

Toothpicks (1 or 2)

Paper plate for glue

Instructions:

1. Fuse mid-weight interfacing to upper shoe.

2. Fuse featherweight interfacing to fabric soles.

3. Cut shoe soles out of medium-weight/heavy cardboard stock. You can use a corrugated box if you have one laying around!

4. **Piping (optional—if you are not using piping, skip to step 5):** Place piping on upper edge of shoe, having the edge of the piping even with the edge of the upper sole. Baste in place. Stitch using a zipper foot. Trim seam allowance on the piping to a scant ¼". Clip piping every ¼".

5. **Upper shoe:** Sew center back seam. Press seam open.

6. **Upper shoe lining:** Sew center back seam. Press seam open.

7. With right sides together, stitch upper edges together. Clip around curves. Turn right side out. Press. Baste raw edges together.

8. Cut a piece of thread 60" long. Fold in half. Thread needle, then fold in half again. You will have four threads. Make a strong knot.

9. Starting at the back of the *upper shoe*, baste around the *lower edge* of the upper shoe. Pull up the basting stitches slightly. Set aside.

10. Starting at *fabric* sole back, baste around the entire outer edge. Pull up the gathering stitches and hold taunt.

11. Holding the right *shoe sole card stock*, place under the fabric sole and pull the gathering stitches tightly, until the fabric is completely "hugging" the cardboard sole. Tie knot securely.

12. Slip the fabric-covered card stock sole into the upper shoe *from the top*. Press down on the card stock sole and gently ease it into the upper shoe. Pull up on the gathering stitches until it hugs the sole. Look at the bottom of the sole. There should be about ¼" of fabric under the card stock, not more than that. Tie knot.

13. Pour about a teaspoon of glue onto a paper plate.

14. Looking at the underside of the sole: Use a toothpick to spread plenty of glue around the entire shoe *under* the seam allowance.

15. Put about 8 clothespins around the shoe to secure the fabric to the sole.

16. In one half hour, check the clothespins by opening *each one* to make sure they are not glued to the shoe. Check all the clothespins in another half hour. Let dry overnight.

17 The next morning, remove clothespins carefully. To remove: If clothespin does not open right away, gently twist back and forth to open, then *push the clothespin toward the center of the shoe to remove.* Use your index finger to go around the inside of the shoe to "open" up the inside (after all, it was squished all night!).

18 **Fabric sole bottom:** Starting at the sole back, baste around the outer edge. Pull up on the gathering stitches until the seam allowance turns under. Press gently.

19 Place the wrong side of the sole to the bottom of the shoe. Pin in place. Adjust gathering to fit. Feel free to use a lot of pins going around the entire shoe! Blind-stitch shoe sole in place. The edge of the fabric sole should come to the edge of the cardboard sole.

20 **Straps (optional):** With right sides together, fold strap in half. Stitch. Turn. Press. Edge stitch ⅛" on both long edges.

21 Even though I have marked strap placement on the pattern, I like to try the shoes on my doll for a perfect fit. I recommend you do the same. It is more accurate since these little shoes could vary slightly. Try the shoe on your doll. Pin the strap on the *inside* of the shoe (inside ankle side). Make sure enough of the strap falls to the inside of the shoe and pin. Hand-stitch in place on both sides of the strap.

22 Bring the strap over the foot to the other side. The straps will be a little long. Turn under a generous ¼" and check for placement. If shoe strap is too long, cut a little, turn under a generous ¼" and check for placement again. (The shoe strap should not be too tight as you want to leave room for socks or tights.)

23 Sew one side of the snap to *strap.* Try the shoe on the doll. Mark placement for the other side of the snap. Sew snap on *shoe.*

24 If you are adding flowers, add them to the shoe while the doll is wearing the shoe. Pin in place, then sew. Add pearls or other embellishments, if desired. We are almost finished!

25 **Bow (optional):** With right sides together, stitch around all four sides.

26 Carefully cut a small slit *on the lining side only,* in the center, about 1" long.

27 Turn inside out. Press.

28 Run a basting stitch in the center. Pull up basting stitch as tight as possible and make a knot.

29 **Bow knot:** Press under ¼" on each side, then fold in half and press.

30 Fold bow knot over center of gathered bow. Turn under raw edge and stitch securely in place.

23 Place bow on shoe. Stitch in place.

23 Add a flower, if desired.

23 Complete these steps for the other shoe and then you will be finished!

23 Great job! That was a lot of work! You should be very proud of yourself!

Pattern

(found in back pocket of book)

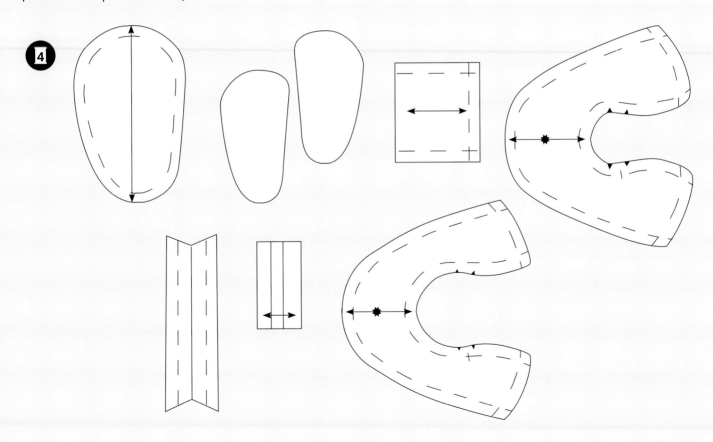

Acknowledgments

I must first thank my husband, Brian, for being instrumental in helping me with this book. I could not have executed any of this without him. He is the most generous man I have ever known. Generous and giving not only of his time, but of his ideas, his words, and loving kindness. Thank you for being supportive of me in every way.

To my editor, Cindy De La Hoz, I wish to say: Thank you, Cindy darling, for believing in me and championing my work! I absolutely loved working with you . . . again! From day one, everything was smooth and effortless, uncomplicated, and straightforward. What a total pleasure!

To Susan Van Horn and Melissa Gerber: Graphic design artists extraordinaire! Thank you for adding stylish beauty to all the pages! Your inspired and inventive designs brought energy and sparkle to *Doll Couture!*

My grateful appreciation to my wonderful family and treasured friends for being so giving of themselves and of their time. Special love and thanks to: Shari Veitsman, Chana Greenberg, Tehila Deutsch, Nancy Lee Moran, Sandra Silverstein, Alex Veitsman, Michael Greenberg, David Greenberg, Elly Greenberg, Alan Meyerson, Adrienne Barrett, Robert and Julia Stein, and Linda Silverstein.

I am especially indebted to my lovely cousin, Mary Meyerson, for her unwavering help during the fun but hectic photo shoot of the *Couture* dolls. She ran around like a hurricane, making certain the girls had all their appropriate accessories and kept a steady stream of dolls ready for their "close-up" in front of the camera.

Special thanks to my photographer, Bryan McCay, for flying in from New York to photograph the "girls." Once again, you "captured" on every image all the love I put into my *Doll Couture* dresses. You are so professional, so kind, so enjoyable to be around. Let's do this again!

Our publisher, Chris Navratil: Thank you for your continued love and support of this book! All the girls send their love and kisses to you!

Notes